GHOST

FIELD JOURNAL
OF A BIRD DOG

CAPT. TONY PETRELLA

Arbutus Press
Traverse City, Michigan

Arbutus Press
Traverse City, Michigan
info@arbutuspress.com
www.Arbutuspress.com

Ghost: Field Journal of a Bird Dog
Copyright © 2012, Capt. Tony Petrella
ISBN - 978-1-933926-43-8

Printed in the United States of America

CONTENTS

DEDICATION

FOR KATE,
Who has always shared my highs and lows with Ghost,
and life.

Foreword

One of the joys of being a full-time outdoors writer is that I get to hunt upland gamebirds with a lot of different people and a lot of different dogs. Along the way I've learned to never, ever criticize a man's choice of a wife, truck or bird dog.

I have seen men who are powerful leaders in industry and politics fawning with pride over some of the most godawful, incompetent mutts ever to disgrace their breed.

And then there are dogs like Ghost, Tony Petrella's English setter, perhaps the most aptly named bird dog I've ever seen, because her skills and intelligence set a standard that can only be called spooky.

A friend who is a professional dog trainer speaks condescendingly of the average hunter's pointers and retrievers as "couch dogs," because they spend 99.9 percent of their time sitting around a house or yard. His dogs live at a hunting preserve where they accompany sports who pay by the bird, and as he likes to point out, "My dogs see more birds in a week than a lot of the couch dogs do in their whole lives."

But Ghost had an advantage over even those preserve dogs. While they hunt confused pheasants and chukars that had been taken from a warm cage and tossed under a bush they were too addled to leave, Ghost knew the sly ways of the wild grouse and woodcock that live in the woodlands around her northern Michigan home.

As I write this our 16-day firearms deer season is on, when 650,000 people go into the woods with shotguns and rifles and the state sensibly shuts down the grouse season until December 1.

The hiatus is a good time to reminisce and let memories of hunts with Tony and Ghost tumble by like autumn leaves in the trout streams we often hunted along.

One of my favorites was a day we hunted grouse by the Manistee River not far from our homes in northern Michigan, and Ghost went on point at a clump of viburnum not 30 seconds after she was taken off the leash.

We walked up and flushed two birds, missed both (hey, it was the early season with a lot of leaves on the trees), and earned the usual "How could you?" look from Ghost.

We did a bit better the rest of the day and got back to the trucks as the unseasonably warm September morning became an afternoon too hot for men and beasts. We unloaded our guns and were putting gear away when Ghost flowed across the ferns to the same clump of trees and went on point again.

Shaking his head, Tony walked over to put the dog on the leash, telling her, "Give it up, Ghost. That's where we flushed those birds when we started."

He hadn't reached the dog when two more grouse burst out of the greenery and soared off while four of us watched them go with unloaded guns in hand.

Ghost was the first in a string of English setters Tony would own when she came as a tiny pup to the log house he and his wife, Kate, had built on the upper Manistee, which along with the nearby Au Sable provides most of his summer income as a trout guide.

But while Tony loves to trout fish and is one of the best and most personable guides I have met in 30 years as an outdoors writer for two of America's biggest newspapers, his passion is those few weeks from mid-September until New Year's, when he and his beloved dogs can hunt the ruffed grouse and woodcock that are found in good numbers from U.S. Highway 10 in the Michigan's Lower Peninsula all the way north to Ironwood, on the Wisconsin border at the far western end of the Upper Peninsula.

Grouse numbers vary from year to year, partly because of a natural grouse cycle that biologists have carefully documented, partly because of varying weather patterns that occasionally bring savage winters where the snow locks down the landscape until well into April, and partly because of habitat changes caused by fluctuations in the demand for timber and paper products.

What never changes is Tony's utter fascination with English setters, because grouse hunting is just an excuse to own them. And what never changed was his special relationship with Ghost.

I've never seen a better setter than Ghost. Sleek and lean and muscular, she was a perfect example of her breed, but her personality was more Meryl Streep than Sandra Bullock. This wasn't the cute, shy girl next door but a dominant, confident lady who didn't hesitate to let other dogs know who was in charge, including her own kennel mates.

She was friendly to just about any human, especially if you were carrying a gun. Once you'd hunted with her a few times, she became absolutely enamoured of you the next time she saw you, rubbing herself against your legs and hand to ensure that she was picked first and most often when it came time to let a dog out to hunt.

Ghost was barely four months old when Tony first left her whining and barking in her cage, furious that she had been left behind while he took the other dogs out to hunt. She had already been introduced to grouse and woodcock wings and other training devices, and at five months he took her out on a leash on a real shoot.

Talking about that first hunt, Tony said, "One guy shot a woodcock that his dog wouldn't touch [many bird dogs apparently detest the odor and taste of woodcock]. So I asked him if he would mind if I tried to get Ghost to retrieve it. She was on it right away, and from then on, it was off to the races. She required less training than any dog I ever owned."

Like most experienced dog trainers, Tony is well aware that people can't teach dogs to hunt. They are born knowing how to do that. What people do is teach the dogs to hunt when and where and in a manner that the people want them to.

Ghost seemed to have figured that part out for herself as well. On days when the grouse were few and far between, we'd hear her bell from hither and yon as she covered huge areas at high speed. But every few minutes she'd come running past and cast an eye at us to make sure we were still doing what we were supposed to, and if Tony let out a whistle through his teeth she responded in seconds.

Tony works his dogs through the summer and fall in the woods near his home, which have excellent grouse and woodcock cover. And when the Michigan hunting seasons close and he and Kate head south, he keeps the dogs working on quail in Florida until the spring days grow too warm.

The result of that training is dogs that know intimately what grouse and woodcock and quail smell like and what they're likely to do when being tracked; dogs that literally live for the opportunity to hunt. Ghost was the epitome of years of such training.

Yet she was also a wonderful companion around the house, especially for Kate in the long weeks when her work as a freelance book editor kept her in Michigan, amid the almost palpable silence of woodlands in the raw days of early spring, while Tony was guiding for tarpon and snook and the saltwater species near their winter home in southwest Florida.

A few weeks ago I saw a T-shirt that bore the slogan "In dog beers I've only had seven." It reminded me of the succession of dogs in my own life and how I wished that some of them were been born with the genetic programming for a lifespan closer to my own. I know that Tony wished the same for Ghost.

As Ghost grew older Tony began to limit her activity, but he wasn't able to blunt her enthusiasm, and even half blind and half deaf she still had a nose that was twice as good as most other dogs.

I sometimes wondered what Ghost must have really thought of us, because when I think about her, a lot of the memories are instances when we failed to live up to the standard she set.

One morning we had gone out for a short hunt in the bottomlands along the river, where Ghost could find lots of birds in a half mile or so. I had managed to step thigh deep into a bog, so I was quite happy when Tony decided that Ghost had done enough and it was time to head back to the house for breakfast.

As we walked along a trail Ghost suddenly pulled off 90 degrees to the right, as far as her leash would let her go, pointing at a downed aspen. We had literally kicked that tree when we walked past it an hour earlier, and Tony tried to pull the dog back, assuring her that nothing was there.

"Okay, satisfy yourself," he said, dropping the leash so she could reach the tree. Instead, she kept going another 20 yards to a second deadfall where two grouse thundered off before she could complete her point.

Naturally, our double barrels were empty and broken over our arms.

And the look of scorn that Ghost gave us could have taken paint off a wall.

Eric Sharp
Outdoors Editor,
Detroit Free Press

INTRODUCTION

If I could only spend one month of the year alive on earth, there's no question it would be October. I revel in the sharp smell of crushed leaves and pine needles on a frosty morning; the gentle whining of dogs trembling with anticipation; the soft, satisfying "chunk" of a truck door when it's time for Dawn Patrol.

Yes, October is very, very special.

That's why there's a particularly warm and grateful place in my heart for the dogs and men who've hunted grouse and woodcock with me during the past 25 years.

I guess I feel privileged, if that's the right word, to tell you about our glorious days of triumph, as well as some humiliating moments of ineptitude. The laughs, as well as some frightening moments of terror. The pure joy of simply being there.

Because good, bad, or ugly, those moments are what make each hunt memorable in its own way.

A blue-ticked Llewellyn setter with thick silky feathering, one white-capped black ear, and amazingly expressive eyes—Manistee River Ghost—is at the center of these stories. Surprisingly enough, all of them are true.

She could be an awfully hardheaded one-man's dog, and always about finding birds that when she was just a kid I sometimes had to chase after her through two counties and across a couple of rivers.

Once, that fanaticism nearly killed her.

Ultimately, she became the most famous English setter in Michigan since the days when her grandfather five generations back—Ghost Train—ruled the hardwood coverts both sides of the Mackinac Bridge.

I've hunted over a lot of other setters, as well as Germans, Brits, Spaniels, and even a couple of Griffons, Cockers, and Wimys. I know I'm going to hurt some feelings and probably make more than a few guys angry when I say that not one of those dogs ever equaled Ghost's sheer determination or ability to find birds.

But if you hunted with her just once you'd have to grudgingly agree. Her intensity was utterly incredible starting the day she was born.

She made her first retrieve—on a woodcock—when she was 21 weeks old. I'll tell you all about that a little bit later on.

As your mind wanders through these pages, I'm certain you'll recall magnificent October days when you, too, glided through squishy, golden aspen leaves in search of grouse. Or wrestled through gnarly streamside tag alders where woodcock live.

Maybe you'll remember the look and feel of a fine double gun; the soft, warm texture of a treasured hunting coat; the joy of good leather boots that fit just right; the unique perfume that only comes from the rich aroma of gun oil, spent powder, and saddle soap.

And, most important of all, I expect you'll remember the luxury of stretching comfortably by the fire—snifter in hand—with those special friends who shared that hard day's hunt with you. The ones who truly made the day memorable.

Yes, I mean the dogs. Because, ultimately, everything we do on those exhilarating October days really is about and because of the dogs. We make them. They make us. Together, we forge a bond that creates our own unique piece of heaven wherever a bird dog runs through our lives.

CHAPTER 1

PAINFUL ENDINGS AND JOYOUS BEGINNINGS

I had owned a half-dozen dogs during the previous 25 years.

Most of them were mutts from the pound. None were hunting dogs in the classic sense of the word, although a terrier named CJ pumped her short little legs for all they were worth until she stumbled over a grouse every once in a while.

I don't know why, but she was crazy about birds. Maybe she simply knew that I was more interested in grouse than the carcass of a dead mole, chipmunk, or rabbit—no matter how hard she'd worked to dig it up.

When she died in my arms at three in the morning on the Fourth of July I wailed like a man possessed. Kate thought I'd lost my mind. Actually, it was just my heart.

I cradled CJ in my arms well past dawn. The colder her body got, the more quieter I became. Finally, Kate sat down next to me and softly said "Call Paul. I know it's the Fourth, but he'll know what to do."

Just over two hours later Paul Mesack, one of Michigan's finest veterinarians and my very good friend, had gently taken CJ from me saying, "I'll call in a couple of days."

I was so still during the 20-mile drive home from Paul's clinic Kate thought I was catatonic. Actually, my brain simply was trying to sort through everything that had happened during the past 12 hours. I was numb.

Sitting in the Jeep, with the world flashing past, I inevitably asked myself the age-old question that arises at times such as those: "Now what?" I didn't know. Not exactly, at that point.

It finally became obvious that since I lived on the banks of the Manistee River, and was surrounded by grouse and woodcock, it was time for me to own a full-fledged bird dog. I'd been "mooching" off my hunting partners long enough.

But what kind of dog? I had hunted over various Germans and Brits and English during the previous several years. Most of them found pheasant, grouse, and woodcock pretty regularly.

"Hell," I thought miserably, "CJ isn't even in the ground and I'm trying to decide on another dog." But, I knew that's what I had to do.

After a whirlwind of talking with several friends, somebody gave me the name and phone number of "a guy who knows a lot about bird dogs." I called him.

He listened patiently to my rambling story and then simply asked, "What is it you want out of your dog?"

That stopped me.

"Well," I said at last, "since bird season is only fifteen percent of the year, I guess I want a buddy as much as anything else. They all find some birds if they have any kind of nose, don't they?"

He didn't hesitate an instant. "Then get an English setter. A German shorthair will tolerate you. Maybe. A Brit will say hello when you come home, then spend the rest of the night in its box. But if you're not petting an English setter, it wants to know WHY!"

I'm not real certain about people who believe in "fate." When I was a kid, the Sisters of The Immaculate Heart of Mary never blinked whenever someone dared question predestination. They just said "Because." Words like "luck," "chance," or "think it through" weren't in the approved IHM handbook.

So it was eerily strange when the following morning I saw a one-inch blurb advertising English Setters For Sale in the weekly shopping guide that was stuck next to our mailbox every Sunday.

A woman's pleasant voice, with a hint of the south, said that a litter had just been whelped and were ready for new homes. Softly setting down the phone, I sighed and looked at Kate. "We're going to Cheboygan tomorrow."

"What time do we leave?" she asked.

"Early. I want to see the pups first thing when the pen is opened."

Incredibly, there was a skim of ice on the bird bath that July morning. A portend? I shuddered. But an hour later I watched a bunch of eight-week-old puppies splash through a tiny spring, laughing and banging into each other and rolling in the water.

Northern Pioneer Patty, of a line descended from the renowned Ghost Train down through Ghost Train's Delight, Ghost Train's Fancy, and Pioneer Ghost, watched her brood with sleepy benevolence.

Induna Oscar, on the other hand, must have been off playing poker with some of his cousins out of the Amos Mosley strain of Llewellyn setters. He'd done his part.

I didn't know it that golden morning, but I had just found the key to the gates of a grouse hunter's equivalent of Fort Knox.

"Patty" had nudged each of her kids outside the door of the enclosure. Grateful, probably, for a few minutes of peace. I, on the other hand, was armed with the obligatory bird wing tied to the tip of a fly rod. As if any puppy of any breed wouldn't be curious enough to pounce on something being fluttered through the dirt.

I resolutely went through the whole routine of flopping the wing, rolling a couple of the pups over, and even holding them down to see how much they'd fight me. "This one," I finally said, and Roni Worrick beamed.

"She'll make a fine bird dog for you," Roni said, not knowing how incredibly prophetic she was. Pure gold. Twenty-four-karat talent.

Like everybody who's ever brought home a puppy, the burning question we had during the hour's drive back to Deward was what to name her.

Spot? Too trite. Rags? Naw, her hair was silky smooth.

Ghost? She raised her head off tiny white front paws and looked at us. We sorta laughed, and tossed out more combinations while she yawned sleepily and blew out sweet puppy breath.

A little while later we came back to "Ghost" and her eyes popped open again. Kate and I sorta looked at each other and didn't laugh quite as much.

By this time we were back home and the pup was lying in the sand underneath the tailgate of my pickup truck. When we said "Ghost" for the third time she looked up inquisitively and squinted at us with her jaw thrust forward. Right then the matter was closed forever.

Manistee River Ghost it would be.

In the Ojibwe tribal language, Ma-nist-ee means "Spirit of the Woods." Over the next decade, she proved beyond doubt that never was a name more fitting for a bird dog living in our little corner of the world.

CHAPTER 2

GHOST'S TOWN TRULY LIVES AGAIN

Before I go any further with these yarns, I suppose you ought to know a little bit about the place where an awful lot of this magical stuff involving dogs and grouse has taken place.

It's called Deward, after a big-money fellow who owned 200,000 acres of white pine forest up here in the northern tip of Michigan's "mitten." They used to call it "cork pine," by the way. Back before the Civil War. The American Civil War.

I'll tell you about him and his epic journey, and all about his town, in a minute. What you need to understand right now is that the place is—appropriately enough—a ghost town.

About the only tangible things left behind are a cluster of gnarled old apple trees and some enormous, half-busted cement footings down near the river where hundred-foot-tall pines became canyon-high stacks of boards.

There's also a poured concrete foundation from what was the communal ice house. And, scattered along the open plain where the main part of town had been, there are a lot of knee-wrenching depressions in the dirt where privies and wells were dug.

But from September of 1901 until March 16, 1912, gigantic saw blades roared almost nonstop. Several wide leather belts turned in sequence, so each one could be serviced without shutting down the line—a concept some guy named Henry Ford put to pretty good use a few years later.

I grew up in northeastern Ohio when Big Steel was at its peak in the fifties and early sixties. Republic Steel, The Carnegie

Works, Youngstown Sheet & Tube turned molten liquid into locomotive engines and Buick bumpers.

Each mill spewed soot into the sky from dozens of smokestacks, and you immediately knew which one a man worked at simply by looking at the soot-stained color of the tires on his car.

They were hard, dangerous places to work. And a man was always dirty, tired, and usually underpaid. Just like at the huge Deward sawmill that had turned northern Michigan into a moonscape thirty-five years before I was born.

Records show that about 175,000 board-feet of lumber were sawed at Deward every day. Sometimes more. More, in fact, than any other mill chewed up at any time, at any place, in the history of the world. The sawyers worked every day but Sunday in 12-hour shifts, and millwrights worked round-the-clock.

A lot of rotting old tree stumps remain, a century later, as mute testimony to their sweat, aching bodies, and curses. Some of the stumps measure more than ten feet around, and in places there are so many they look like headstones in a cemetery.

Deward's lumberjacks and railroad men rebuilt Chicago after its "Great Fire," plus a whole lot of eastern Wisconsin and a big swath of northern Michigan that was incinerated at the same time. One entire season's worth of lumber was even shipped all the way to Argentina for some reason that's been lost in the fog of history.

The ironic thing those loggers didn't know, or probably wouldn't have cared about, is that by earning their daily bread cutting down every last "Monarch" white pine, they also helped create what ultimately would become some of the finest grouse habitat anywhere in the United States.

Once the forest canopy opened, low-bush blueberries—also called huckleberries by the locals—started covering the sandy soil.

Wild strawberries, wintergreen, and blackberry canes came next. Poplar, chokecherry, and pin-oak trees eventually provided catkins and acorns for winter food, and the grouse population flourished.

The new sunshine let viburnum bushes and tag alders sprout along the banks of the Manistee River, and woodcock migrating south from Canada and Michigan's Upper Peninsula had a safe refuge where they could stop for a few days and rest their wings.

Some liked the place well enough to make a permanent home.

Meanwhile, with every tree that fell, those tough old Swede sawyers, wiry French log-runners, and displaced New England railroaders were in the process of losing their own homes.

When the final whistle blew, most of them dismantled their houses' clapboard siding and piled it, along with doors, windows, furniture, and children onto wagons.

They left Deward forever and headed off to the next camp of opportunity.

The two-room school, boardinghouse, company store, even the Swedish Lutheran Church—built with company lumber and loggers' labor at night—vanished.

Mrs. John Olson was the last to leave, in August of 1932, and Deward (he had always signed his name D. E. Ward) became a quiet piece of Michigan's history.

Curiously, there had been a standoffish segregation of sorts in Deward.

The railroad men and their families all clustered in houses near the Detroit & Cheboygan roundhouse and engine repair shop, which D. E. Ward conveniently owned, on the knoll at the south end of town.

Most all of the bosses lived on the far northwest side, across the dirt road from the church and school, in a line of houses called "White Collar Row." They apparently were a little "clubbier" and must have got along pretty well.

Everybody else—about 800 people at the town's peak—lived somewhere in the middle, in one of the 300 cottages the company had let them throw together, or rent. Four rooms were $4 a month. Five rooms, five bucks.

The loggers and railroad men even had their own baseball teams. There's no record of who won the most games, but players and fans had to walk more than six miles to the saloon and whorehouse in Frederic to pay off their bets. Deward was a "clean" camp.

Getting back to those little cottages. The funny thing about their outhouses is that the townsfolk who lived here tossed pieces of now-unrecognizable metal and all sorts of broken crockery down the shafts, which had been shored up with bricks hauled in from the Saginaw Brick Company.

Some shards of dishes and bowls they left in the ground have such beautifully delicate patterns the woman of the house must have wept bitterly for their loss.

Fifty years after Mrs. Olson gave up and left Deward, guys with metal detectors swept through and dug up all of those old privies looking for treasure that might have inconveniently dropped out of a man's pants pocket.

Oh, well. The good news for me and Kate is that about a hundred of those bricks became the fireplace hearth and fascia when we built our house along the Manistee River just five miles north of Ghost's town.

It's, I don't know, a feeling of sorta being connected to
those folks and their rough daily lives when I look at the mix of
reddish, tan, or cream-colored bricks and know they're more than
a hundred years old. Some of them are a bit crumbly around the
edges. Others still boldly display the SBC logotype.

Most of the loggers, locomotive drivers, rail-splitters,
maybe even the schoolmarms who worked at the camp, died before
I was born. I've never met anyone whose family lived there, or
heard of any reunion of folks who sweated and prayed and raised
their children amid summer's blackflies or the bitter cold and deep
winter snow of Deward.

And yet, I often wonder if they know what that river, that
land, means to so many trout anglers and upland hunters throughout Michigan and even around the world.

I wonder if they know that because of what they did in
their ghost town, a hundred years later another Ghost would run
through it. And that her name, like that of David E. Ward, would
live forever.

Our log house, which we nicknamed Tapa-Wing-It, is filled with mementoes from and about the people who made my years with Ghost such a pleasure.

CHAPTER 3

GLORIOUS MEMORIES OF DAYS GONE BY

Damn these old Christmas cards!

Kate's off in the woods with Ghost and Heart. I'm in front of a roaring fire with ghosts and a heavy heart. The house is simply overflowing with memories of people and places, and sometimes they're damned hard for me to deal with very well.

Sinking deeper into my favorite chair after tossing another log onto the grate, I wrapped myself in the woven "fish" blanket Bill Halliday gave us and looked around the greatroom.

From its spot above the mantel, Jean Woodbury's needlework trout is splashing water all over the hand-carved manatee I found at a small roadside stand in Islamorada.

The richly colored cloisonné that John Norcross brought back from his last trip to France—the one that wiped out most of our final bird-hunting season—is still painful to look at.

There's a Summers fly rod in a cherrywood holder he made especially for it, and a bamboo rod I made for Kate 30 years ago is laying on the mantel.

Lots of Ruimveld prints are on the walls, along with a bunch by Corey, Langdon, and Cleary. And a caricature of me with Larry Czonka and Jim Kiick that Pulitzer Prize winner Sam Rawls sketched when I left the Palm Beach *Post*.

I had orders from Kate to sort through a whole mess of things we've bought, found, and been given during more than 40 years together. She wants organization in the house these last few days before deer camp "because then it's butchering and packing before we leave for Florida."

So here I am with heavy boxes in my hands and memories in my mind. Damn these old Christmas cards.

"You've got to LEAD those birds!" I could hear The Colonel yelling at me, then sadly adding, "You won't be knocking down many birds over your dog this fall shooting like that, my boy!"

With a disgusted shake of his head, John Norcross flipped his wrist and grimaced at the usual cast of skeet range loungers. "These pups just won't *listen*!"

I thought he was going to snatch the Beretta out of my hands right there at station six.

Fortunately, I busted the last eight clays and The Colonel positively beamed. "THAT'S the way to do it," he yelled. Everybody smiled. Even me. "Let's go drink a glass of wine."

Now he was dead and I vaguely remember mumbling some half-assed sort of eulogy at his funeral. I was in an absolute stupor that awful day.

A week later I found out that Dick Beardsley, my best friend since our days as sportswriters in Atlanta, had died of a brain aneurysm out in Washington. "Just like CJ," I remember thinking.

It was too much to absorb. I grabbed a rod from the rack, walked down to the river, and went fishing. Both of them would understand because both of them were with me.

Even though Dick's idea of "fishing" was busting open crab claws, or better yet a lobster, he was a great guy to have around on a bird hunting or fishing trip.

He'd pack that big old pipe of his with foul Arabian tobacco that made a goat smell good, twirl his greased handlebar mustaches, and utter some piercingly poignant commentary about life in These United States. Plus, he always brought good wine.

Dick was a great friend.

The Colonel, on the other hand, would bellow from the stern of my Au Sable Longboat as I poked through different fly boxes. "The only fly you need to catch these big browns is Jerry's Drake," he'd yell. "Dammit! Do you want to catch fish or NOT?"

I missed the hell out of both of them, and was thoroughly miserable all of that summer.

The bird season that was closing in a couple of days was a whole lot worse. Every time I hunted with John's son, Marc, or Bob Popp, or Rex Farver or John David Korte, one of us—sooner or later—would sigh "I sure do miss that crusty old bastard! It just ain't the same."

One of the things I really missed most was getting John steamed up. Just for the helluvit.

He'd sputter and snort and carry on something awful whenever I'd contradict his opinion on anything from fishing to politics. Then I'd laugh like hell and a boyish grin would spread across his face. "Okay. Okay," he'd say. "Ya got me that time. Dammit!"

Early in our friendship, we'd take turns poling either his boat or mine while the other fished. As he neared 80 his steering got so erratic I often had to claw my way out of streamside tag alders. So, I started doing all the pushing.

John fussed and grumbled about not wanting to hog the fishing, but I figured since I was 30 years younger I could stand the chaff. And it was safer.

His favorite haunt was the upper Manistee River just west of Grayling. It was there, usually during black starless nights in June, he'd quietly spin his stories while we waited for *Hexagenia limbata* mayflies to hatch or fall.

Tales of blue water off Chesapeake Bay on big boats and high seas. Memories of tiny creeks and huge brook trout in the gnarled forests of Michigan's Upper Peninsula. Reminiscences about Duke, the Llewellyn before Ben, that still made him clear his throat.

Then a crash like somebody throwing a bowling ball into the river would stop John's story in mid-sentence. "My boy," he'd say, "that was a very large brown trout. Ease the boat downriver a bit. And be QUIET about it. Dammit!"

He called me "Sarge" because of my dogged get-it-done thoroughness. So, I told him if I was "Sarge," he certainly must be "The Colonel," despite the fact he'd actually been a Navy Lieutenant (jg) during World War II.

And you know, with all the stories I heard during those dark nights, he never did tell me about that morning in the South Pacific when he won the Distinguished Flying Cross.

Only once, after I saw his medal in a shadowbox, did I probe for details. His non-reply was simple and direct. "There's a big fish under that logjam downstream on the right. I don't think you can listen and pole at the same time. Pole, my boy. Pole." I poled.

We jammed a lot of hunting and fishing into a relatively short time. "I wish I'd met you 30 years ago," he once said to me while we were putting away the shotguns. For a guy who makes his living with words, I was shocked to find that I was at a loss for any.

The Colonel had a special cackle in his laugh as he watched Ghost grow into a grouse hunter. "Look at that little dog gooooo!" he'd yell, and nicknamed her "The Cheboygan Comet."

Ghost found out how to point and retrieve that first season under John's watchful and usually critical eye. She even taught herself to backstand Ben's points, and usually gave him an awful lot of respect.

But the first time I killed a pheasant that she considered "our" bird Ghost rudely shouldered Ben aside, picked it up and ran in a tight half-circle. Then she set the pheasant on the grass and lay down with her chin on it.

We both learned a lot. She from Ben. I from The Colonel. In fact, I still think of him every time I fish the Manistee above CCC Bridge, or when the dogs and I hunt the places he taught us to love.

The memories are especially bright as I wander through the logbook and remember the fish we caught or lost. The tough shots we made. The easy ones we missed. All of the things that made our days afield so special, and enriched mine so much.

The printed message on The Colonel's last card read: *"Christmastime is a time for reflecting on joys that we've known all year through. And for thinking of people who mean so very much—it's a time for remembering you."*

You, too, Colonel. You, too.

Ghost was all smiles on her first hunt, October 5, 1997, when we joined Doug Truax along the banks of the Manistee River near the CCC Bridge.

CHAPTER 4

THE PRELIMINARIES ARE OVER—TIME TO HUNT

It was brilliantly sunny and 81 degrees on October 5, 1997, when Ghost went hunting for the first time. Neither one of us knew what to expect, but we both were pretty excited despite the suffocating heat.

I had first met Doug Truax several years before, when he worked for Orvis. Now he was senior editor at Countrysport Press in Traverse City, and had recently hired me to sell its books and artwork to fly fishing shops in the Midwest.

We had never hunted together. But Doug had a four-year-old Llewellyn setter named Tess, and naturally I'd been talking nonstop about my new puppy. Ghost was 20 weeks old when we decided to look for some birds.

The dogs got to know each other that morning in the way dogs usually do, while Doug and I commiserated about the heat. After a bit, our mutual friend Bob Summers, who lives in Traverse City and builds world-famous bamboo fly rods, finally pulled up.

It was time for Ghost to learn the game.

One of the "books" I was peddling for Countrysport at the time was a handsome maroon three-ring binder filled with heavy cream-colored pages. Each one has a very nice sepia line-drawing of a gamebird or hunting dog, and pre-printed places for recording the details of the day's hunt.

It's a pretty classy thing, and I'm sorry to say Countrysport quit producing them. Fortunately, I snapped up a few extras way-back-when, and more recently Kate managed to find some additional binders and pages as a Christmas gift for me.

Anyway, after Ghost and I got home that afternoon I recorded the who/what/where/when of our historic day. Which means, essentially, everything that happened.

Reading it all these years later, what I wrote while Ghost and I were waiting for Doug and Bob sounds like the nervous drivel of a guy taking his kid to the first day of school. Actually, I guess it was.

"My Little Girl has gone through all of the usual stuff with rags on the end of fly rods to find out if she'll point (she does). I banged pots and pans while she was eating, and fired a cap gun to see if it would scare her (it didn't)."

Kate even helped monitor Ghost's reaction when I walked 400 yards from the house and fired a .22 pistol. I worked my way progressively closer to the house with each shot and talked with Kate on our hand-held radios. *"Nothing. She just wants to see where you are. She's standing on the window seat in the dining room. Watching you."*

We took it slow and easy with Ghost, looking for the slightest indication of fear. I hope you've never owned a gun-shy dog, because it's just about the most miserable experience there is for a wanna-be hunter and his dispirited woulda-been hunting dog. One of my cousins ruined a shorthair puppy years ago, and it was a damned sad sight.

As I recall, without any preamble whatsoever he took it out to a pheasant lease and cut loose with his unplugged 12 bore. From then on, the very sight of a shotgun made that poor dog tremble and hide.

I was inexperienced about this business of training bird dogs. But knew I had to get it right.

Actually, according to my logbook, some fellows hunting across the river from my house were the ones who cemented the deal for me. Each time they shot, Ghost perked her ears and looked intently in the direction of the noise. And whined in anticipation.

Unfortunately, my log also shows that even though the rest of us were wildly enthusiastic on that hot October morning, the birds mostly declined to participate in the fun.

Doug held off on shooting at a woodcock that flushed wild, hoping for a point from Tess or Ghost on the follow-up, but we never did find where that bird sat down. Later, Bob missed a grouse flush. Then another woodcock flew off unmolested amid the flutter of wings and that "peeeet" they make. That was it.

Truth be told, I don't think Ghost had a firm grasp on what she was there for. At that particular moment she seemed perfectly happy to chase Tess, investigate strange new woodland smells, and simply run free through the jumble of cedars, popple, and tag alders.

All that changed one week later.

I was with The Colonel, his crunchy old pal Bob Popp, from Luzerne (halfway between Grayling and Mio), and John David Korte, from Indiana. Ben was laid up with a cut paw, so JD's setter, Molly, did all the work. Ghost mostly watched.

It was another one of those hot, sunny days when we should have been floating the Manistee and casting 'hopper patterns to big brown trout. Scent was scarce. Finally, a woodcock spooked and John David miraculously knocked it down.

"Fetch," he told Molly.

She trotted over to the dead bird, sniffed it, and turned away. "Fetch," JD said again. Molly sat down and tugged a burr from her right front leg. "Fetch," JD said, more forcefully. Molly spat out the burr and stared at him.

"Uh, John David," I said, haltingly. "Would you mind if I let Ghost retrieve that bird?"

"Go ahead," he replied. "Molly sure don't want anything to do with it."

I can't remember right now if I said "fetch" or "dead bird" or just something mundane like "get it, Ghost." That part's not in my logbook. But she stared at me curiously, looked at the dead bird, then bounded over and snatched it off the ground.

Well. The fuss I made over Ghost would have caused you to believe that no other dog in the history of Creation had ever done anything as wonderful as her picking up that woodcock.

"Good Girl!" I must have repeated it a dozen times as I rubbed her all over and kissed her face while I tried to pry the bird from her mouth. "We'll work on the give-it part later," I said to the guys. Alas, that was wishful thinking on my part.

Finally, Norcross had enough. "I'm hungry," he grumbled. "Let's go eat."

Between bites of venison sausage, crisp apples, and some of Kate's world-famous chocolate chip cookies, JD told me to take Ghost off to the far side of my truck "so she can't see what I'm doing."

A couple of minutes later he yelled. "Bring her out here and let's see if she can find that woodcock again."

I patted Ghost's head and whispered, "Okay, find 'em!" And, she did.

"Tony," JD said as Ghost first went on point, then grabbed the bird, "I wanna buy that dog."

I laughed, hugged Ghost, and tugged gently at the woodcock in her mouth.

"I'm serious," he continued. "I wanna buy Ghost."

"Sorry, John David. She's not for sale."

I was off somewhere in Illinois or Ohio, visiting fly shops and talking about rods or waders or something like that, the next week when John David called.

"You don't know me," he told Kate, "but I hunted with Tony and John Norcross last Saturday. I want to buy Ghost."

"Um, I'm pretty sure Tony's not interested in selling her."

"I'll give you four thousand dollars for her."

"That's a lot of money for a dog," Kate replied, "but I still don't think he'll sell her."

"I'll go to forty-five hundred but that's the best I can do. My wife's standing right here next to me."

"I'll tell him when he gets home, John, but I'm pretty sure I know what his answer will be."

JD became a good friend of mine over the ensuing years. We've hunted together many times, and shared liquor, good food, and plenty of laughs. John Norcross is gone now. So are Ben and Molly.

Ghost remains. A classic fixture in northern Michigan's grouse coverts and woodcock bogs. And every time we hunt together I'll sidle up to JD and say, "Ya know, you're a pretty lucky guy!"

"Why's that?" he'll invariably reply.

"Because," I tell him, "you saved forty-five-hundred bucks and STILL get to hunt over Ghost!"

Every upland hunter dreams of the day his dog will make its first point, and retrieve, on a ruffed grouse. Ghost made hers when she was six months old and from that day forward became an incredible bird-finding machine.

CHAPTER 5

No Longer a Virgin

In the movie *Ghost,* after the gun smoke had wafted away on the night air, a host of golden, beatific angels came to escort Patrick Swayze into heaven. "Unchained Melody" swelled to a gentle crescendo.

In real life, after the gun smoke had drifted away in the gray morning mist, I was metaphorically escorted into heaven by an unhappy ruffed grouse. The only music was my Ghost's gentle whine of rapture.

We had hunted along the Au Sable River down around Connor Flat just after dawn. It was drizzly and overcast then, and the purplish oak, brilliant gold aspen, and red viburnum leaves made a soft squishy sound underfoot.

Water dripped from the tips of Ghost's ears, and her tail feathering was a white mess of hair when she went on point the very first time. We were in a small opening in the dark green pines, and it was a little bit misty, like fading smoke on a battlefield. But she had a snootful of bird.

I was so nervous I might as well have been picking my way through claymores as I minced up alongside her. Finally, a soft little shuffling of my boot was all that woodcock could stand and it twittered into the air.

BOOM! My Ghost never flinched. Neither did the woodcock, which corkscrewed through the trees with that telltale flight signature that long ago earned them the nickname "Timberdoodle." I sighed and looked down at Ghost, who still hadn't moved.

"Okay, girl" I said quietly. "Let's go. That one got away."

Ghost nodded and crept forward. Actually, she was awfully polite about the shameful way I had missed that bird. Of course, she was still very young and didn't know enough to be upset with me. That would come later.

She wove her way through the wet weeds and fallen limbs, stopping every once in a while to shake vigorously, snort, and try for another whiff of bird. When she found it she turned into a magazine ad.

You've seen them. Every hair on legs and tail plastered flat from the rain. Head stretched forward. Tail arched skyward. One front paw (always the one nearest the photographer for maximum effect) pulled up high. Body tensed. Anticipation in every fiber of her being.

Ever so slowly, Ghost's eyes shifted sideways to look at me. Then they snapped forward and it was business. I took a step, the bird flew, and the shotgun came up. Of course, I missed it.

By now, Tim Hart, who was acting as the guide since we were on his property, and Neil Burrows, John Norcross' son-in-law, had drifted close to watch the tableau play out. Neither one said a word.

Ghost simply slid her eyes sideways again in what would become her signature expression of disgust until I finally learned how to properly handle a double gun.

I guess I was pretty relieved when the rain really started pouring down about then. I didn't know how much of this excitement leavened with humiliation I could stand. But I had to practically drag Ghost back to the truck.

Steam was rising off her back when I finally got her onto the liftgate and started toweling her down. She was smiling and her tongue was hanging out the left side of her mouth and those big darting eyes were shiny. Water was running down my spine from inside the collar of my wax cotton jacket.

About two hours later, Neil and I pulled into a spot along-side the Manistee River where Kate and I have caught plenty of trout. It's about a mile downstream from the old Deward lumber camp ghost town, and it had always looked pretty "birdy" to me.

Everybody was refreshed. We'd had a lunch of cappacolla on slabs of thick, crusty Italian bread, with generous slices of pro-volone. Ghost and Ben each had wolfed down a handful of high-protein snacks.

Eventually, everybody was ready for more hunting.

The question in my mind, however, was inescapable. Was I ready to finally do my part?

I guess I never will know the answer to that. Not really. The only thing that's absolutely certain is that Ghost pointed her first grouse about 30 minutes after we cut through the red pines and got down near the riverbank.

She and Ben had been criss-crossing through the blackberry canes, beaver-cuts, and thick weeds that make that stretch of the river such a fine place to look for birds.

Finally, they found them.

Neil was behind Ghost. Ben was on her left, along the river. Both he and Ghost were rock solid. She on point, he backstanding.

"Here's your dog, now," Neil said in his lilting New Zea-lander. I was a bit to the right, and didn't get it for a second or two. Then I looked at the three of them and said I'd be right along. "You move up a bit more, and I'll swing in from here."

"Right," was all Neil said. He took a couple of steps. Ben raised a paw. Ghost quivered just a little bit and her feathers—dry now—floated gently in the breeze. I inhaled deeply.

Rather comically, I thought, the grouse popped straight into the air like a jack-in-the-box and perched on the limb of a pale gold tamarack. It teetered just a little bit, and looked puzzled.

We all sort of resembled that old, very old, E. F. Hutton television commercial. The one where a well-heeled guy would tell his pal "My broker is E. F. Hutton. And..." everybody in the restaurant stopped in mid-chew and leaned forward to get the straight scoop.

Yeah, we were just like that. Neil and I stared at each other. Ben was frozen. Ghost stared up at the bird. The grouse looked down at Neil, then at me, then at Ghost—not quite certain what should happen next. So, it flew away.

Tried to, anyway.

"Got him!" I yelled and ran forward. Ghost had picked up the grouse and was carrying around her prize. "We got him, Ghost!" I said, hugging her.

In retrospect, it's more than probable that Neil was the one who actually shot that grouse. In the enthusiasm of the moment, however, there was absolutely no doubt in my mind that I had killed it.

Who knows. Who cares. What mattered most at that instant was the simple fact that Ghost had pointed her first grouse and now she had it in her mouth and we were a couple of very happy hunting partners.

Neil smiled at us. All he said was, "Good shot, mate."

I suppose the most poignant aspect about that bit of drama—forever frozen in my memory—is that it happened directly across the river from where CJ's ashes had been scattered under a huge white pine four months before.

My ashes will go into the river there, and at the base of that ancient tree. Ghost will be with me. Along with CJ, Ben, and Heart. The new puppy, Tug, and even another setter or two—if my time allows—will be there, too. The whole pack of us will forever roam the deadfalls and tag alders of Deward. Looking for grouse and woodcock.

And maybe, just maybe, if I'm in Kate's good graces when it finally happens, bolted to that tree there might even be a small plaque that reads:

"Home is the hunter
Home in the woods.
And the angler
Home in the stream."

Even the best of dogs get hard-headed at age two and Ghost certainly was a prime example of that aggravating phenomenon.

Chapter 6

The Curse of the "Terrible Twos"

I suppose my indoctrination into the real world of English setters came on the opening day of Ghost's second season. The first line in my logbook dated September 20, 1998 is brief.

"A Calamity."

I had decided to start the year at the same place we got her first grouse, in front of "our" final resting place. I was full of memories and great expectations. Humph! Great Expectations. She was a Pip alright.

Ghost hit the ground running that morning and never once looked back. I finally caught up with her about a half-mile downstream. She was on the riverbank. I was on a knoll.

Still pretty much out of breath from my lurching jog through the trees, I managed to wheeze out something that sounded like "Rot 'ere. Rot 'ere!"

Right.

Ghost ignored me and slipped into the river like a cottonmouth. She swam to the opposite bank, paused long enough to shake all over, and went on her own private bird hunt.

After about an hour of calling and whistling, and maybe a little desperate pleading, I gave up and waded across the river in my 17-inch-high Leather Lace-up Boots. Was the water cold? Yes. Was I steaming? Absolutely!

Ghost actually looked a little bit contrite when I followed the collar's beeping and found her lying down in the deer moss, chest heaving and panting hard. I snapped on the leash and resolutely marched her back through the river.

"The Silent Treatment," I decided, as freezing water got waist-high and played the bongo drums with my…well, you understand. "I'll give her The Silent Treatment. She won't be able to stand the absence of my love and affection."

It didn't work. Not then and never any time afterward when she got like that. Have I mentioned she could be a real hard-head?

Because one of us was responsible for buying the groceries—and way back then she never kicked in a nickel—I tended to business the next several days making nonstop phone calls and visiting fly shops. It was nearly two weeks before I took Ghost hunting again.

Naturally, I was apprehensive, but the hunt started well. I dropped a woodcock over her, and we both were pretty giddy about that. I actually started to think that maybe everything was going to be just fine.

When we went to the next covert, my mistake was going back to the spot of our opening day "episode." Silly me. I thought she'd learned her lesson. Instead, she crashed out of the gate like Secretariat at The Derby and was gone just as fast.

I'll cut to the chase and simply say that Kate was looking down from her upstairs office window when I climbed out of the truck two hours later wearing nothing but a shirt. Yeah, again.

Kate watched me wring out my pants and skivvies, and dump about a gallon of water out of my boots. Putting a hand over her eyes, she shook her head mournfully and met me at the kitchen door with a hug.

Since then, I've shared a cup, sighs, and similar horror stories with other upland bird hunters. It doesn't seem to matter what the breed. Dogs are dogs and they all go through "The Terrible Twos." Apparently, it's inevitable. But not one damned bit of fun!

Ghost alternated between beautiful points for me and selfishly hunting for herself the rest of that year. Or, as Kate was beginning to say, "Which Ghost do you think is going to show up today?"

Sometimes she found birds. Other times, it was all I could do to find Ghost.

So, after spending the winter in Florida, working every day on training commands, I fretted throughout spring and summer. All I could think about was, "What will this third hunting season bring?"

To tell the absolute truth, by opening day I was pretty much a nervous wreck.

So, it was with complete astonishment that I began Chapter Three of the logbook by writing, "Ghost was spectacular."

She pointed five woodcock and two grouse the first day out. Five more points the next day, and another six the following morning.

Birds were falling from the sky like meteors, and she was hunting close to me like a seasoned pro. Our team was red hot.

Alas, I was totally delusional.

After all of those perfect hours in the field, we struck out (figuratively and literally) on yet another glorious October morning along the Manistee River. And, yes, I'll be damned to hell if it wasn't once again in that same cursed spot that makes her so wild. No wonder I'll be "buried" there!

Ghost had been stamping her front paws impatiently while I buckled on her beeper and bell. She vaulted out of the Tahoe like a Redstone Rocket. Or, as Norcross used to call her, "The Cheboygan Comet."

I followed lamely, calling "Whoa! Whoa! Ghost, RIGHT HERE! WHOA!!!" I might as well have been speaking Chinese to an oak tree for all the good it did me. Ghost was gone. Period.

Okay. I understand that sometimes the Ying overwhelms the Yang, or something like that. I dunno. I never could keep them straight.

What I do know for certain is the fact that I had committed the Cardinal Sin of bird dog owners. Because she had been performing so beautifully, I'd been bragging about Ghost's skill to John David Korte, Rex Farver, and his son, Chris.

Wow. They certainly got an eyeful. To tell it plainly, she thumbed her nose at me. Again. Swam across the river. Again. And went off to hunt for herself. Again.

Rex and Chris were trying real hard to keep from laughing out loud, but JD was beside himself with glee. Remember, this is the same guy who offered to pay $4,500 for Ghost two years before.

To make matters worse, JD had brought along a very expensive, very German, very powerful camera to record the hunt for posterity.

What he ultimately recorded was my posterior for posterity as I waded the river in my hunting clothes, hat in one hand and shotgun in the other.

Eight months later, at a gathering of Trout Bums in Grayling, John David fulfilled the threat he'd made as I waded through the river that October day. He'd had that photograph printed in two very embarrassing formats, and put them up at auction in the Trout Bum BBQ fundraiser.

The first is a horizontal poster of me in midstream, surrounded by the superimposed heads of taunting trout yelling: "Hey, Lefty Kreh! Over here!" The other is a life-size cutout of me wiping my brow with my shirtsleeve, hat in one hand, shotgun in the other. With a very resigned expression on my face. Anguish is maybe a better word.

It took quite a few years, but I finally managed to become the owner of those priceless pieces of humiliation. I hung the poster in my bedroom, where I can look at it every night.

I don't think I'm going to tell you what I did with the cutout. You'd never believe it, anyway!

Even with nine stitches in her right leg, Ghost was having too much fun at Steve Sendek's camp in Iron River to let a minor thing like that stop her.

Chapter 7

Blood, Blood Everywhere

As I sit in my big leather chair, wine glass at hand and two tired setters at my feet, I'm struck by what a miracle it is that either Ghost or I survived her first few hunting seasons.

A week to the day after Ghost embarrassed me in front of JD and the Farvers by swimming across the river, she impaled a two-inch-long, quarter-inch-thick stick into the soft part of her right elbow.

It was the first of many, many visits to Paul Mesack and the Grayling Hospital for Animals. "Minor," Paul said after pulling out the wood and touching up the hole with Super Glue. "No reason she can't keep hunting."

So, next day we went out with Marc Norcross and his father's setter, Ben. We trudged up and down the hills, trying our best to keep up with the dogs—who were trying their best to outdo each other.

"Upstart pup," I heard Ben growl. "Grumpy old man," Ghost shot back. And so it went for nearly two hours until the overcast turned to mist, and the mist turned to a cold, stinging spray.

Finally, Marc and I looked at each other, shrugged, and whistled for the dogs. Much to my surprise, Ghost trotted up alongside Ben.

We got 20 yards down the old dirt road when Ghost stopped.

"C'mon," I told her. She stood rigid, staring at me. Then she started shivering. The kind of shiver that you just know is reaching way down deep into her bones. And so, for the first time in her young life, I carried Ghost from the field. Marc carried my shotgun.

"Borderline hypothermia," Paul said after doing a double-take when he saw us walk into the clinic. "Keep warm air blowing on her inside the truck and she'll be fine by the time you get home."

Over the years, "What's wrong with her TODAY?" became an all-too-common question around there. Barbed-wire punctures. Scraped eyeballs. A couple hundred foxtail seeds corkscrewing into her skin like porcupine quills. Ghost endured it all.

We went nearly a month after her bout of hypothermia before our run of injury-free days ended.

I had driven six hours to the far western reaches of Michigan's Uper Peninsula, near Iron River. My pal Steve Sendek has a hunting and fishing camp there, so far off the beaten path that some wiseguy in state government decided it would be ideal to build a penitentiary just down the road.

I guess he figured nobody would know, care, or ever go to such an isolated place except to claim a body—dead or alive.

During the years Ghost and I hunted there we heard wild—sometimes maniacal—howling in the middle of the night. She and I discussed it some, but never quite decided if that hideous noise came from four-legged or two-legged animals.

Anyway, at first light we were out in the wispy fog, high-stepping over fallen cedars and oak slashings. It wasn't long before Ghost locked up on a grouse that was parading back and forth on a stout log, strutting and blowing.

He put on quite a show for us, and it reminded me of a particular bantam rooster my grandma had down on the farm when I was a kid. We ate him one Sunday dinner and he was as stringy as burlap.

I never got the chance to taste this fellow. I couldn't shoot without hitting Ghost, and the bird eventually whirred up into a cedar tree.

That's called a "Yooper Point" in those parts, by the way. As in: "Ole, if ya ain't gone ta shoot dat bird, ya best gid outten da way a me gun!" Being of high moral fiber I resisted all of Ghost's pleas. She even offered to shoot it for me, but I declined.

I'm just a little bit ashamed to admit that I did chunk a few sticks at it, but the cheeky bugger simply sneaked further back into the boughs, nipping at some tasty greens before hiding in a crotch near the trunk.

Ghost finally got tired of the nonsense and ran off to find a more pliant playmate. With my arm cocked for another throw I saw Steve about 20 yards away. "I'll make a Yooper outa you yet!" he yelled. "You're gettin' close. Real close."

Dropping the stick as if it was a rattler, I broke open my 20 bore and went off to the sound of Ghost's beeper. She had pinned another grouse, which arm-wrestled its way through some skinny little pine seedlings and dead branches as I walked up.

I hurriedly closed the Beretta and swung on the bird. Ghost gritted her teeth in misery when my double-boom—well, let's just say I disappointed the dog.

So I guess I wasn't really surprised when Ghost took off down the old logging road a few minutes later. Looking for a better wing-shot, I supposed. Oh, I whistled and called for her to come back, but I didn't really expect she would. Not for a while, anyway.

I hunted with Steve and one of his shorthairs for maybe 45 minutes, and finally there she was, about 20 yards off. A silent white ghost alternately staring at me and licking at her right paw.

"Right here!" I said sternly.

Ghost sorta cocked her head, gave her leg another lick, and hobbled over to me. Then I saw the blood.

It covered her right front foot and half of her leg. Raw red skin and white fur flapped like a flag on the Fourth of July.

I whistled. As best I ever can manage a whistle, anyway. Steve stopped walking and looked back. I waved. "Need some help here, buddy."

Once again, I carried Ghost from the field. Steve carried my shotgun.

Steve had grown up with the local vet, whose office is just a mile past the penitentiary, so Doc told us to come "straightaway."

When we got there, I noticed stout bars on his windows and doors. Depending upon which animals want in or out, I supposed.

"Come back in four hours," Doc said after a quick look-see. I did. Nine stitches and a measly fifty bucks later, Ghost wobbled back into my arms and officially onto the PUP list—NFL-speak for "physically unable to perform."

Time drags on inexorably when a hunting dog can't. The quietly flopping tail, the soft whine, the irritated stamping of frustrated paws is rough on beast and man.

Ten days after her doctoring, I sat on a window seat in the kitchen and stared down at Ghost, who was stretched out on the floor in front of the stove.

She looked back with an expression only an aristocratic setter could have learned from England's Grande Dames during Waterloo, Dunkirk, or The Blitz.

Ghost tentatively licked her wound and resolutely stood, raising her chin in a mixture of hope, arrogance, and defiance. With just enough pleading in those expressive eyes to melt my heart. Mrs. Miniver would have been proud.

It had been a tumultuous hunting season and this was the last day. Kate stared at me. Ghost stared at me. My brain screamed *nonono*.

I gave in and took her to the truck.

Manistee River Road was dry and dusty when I drove home three hours later. A fine yellow powder coated the windshield like the pink Pepto-Bismol would do to my insides real soon.

Ghost had been terrible.

"Shouldn't have done it!" I kept repeating to myself. "She was laid up too long and had too much energy. She wouldn't stop running. What a way to end the season. Dammit! Dammit! Dammit!"

Up ahead, a grouse scooted into the road. It strutted and preened for a couple seconds, then ran into the weeds. I stopped so hard that Ghost banged into the side of her crate and asked me none-too-politely what the hell I was doing.

Without answering, I pulled onto an old logging road and turned off the ignition. "It's up to you, kid." Leash. Beeper. Bell. Then Ghost was loose. Running and sniffing, with determination on her face.

I whistled and prayed. She stopped, turned, and ran back into my loving arms. "Good girl, that's perfect," I told her. Then, "Okay, let's go!" and off she went again.

She quartered back and forth, jumping over and around deadfalls until it looked like she was getting too far out. I whistled. "Right here!" And she did.

About then, I remembered W. C. Fields' great old line, and figured the best I could hope for was an even break. "Time to go home on a high note," I thought.

But before I could leash her, Ghost took three very slow steps into a little copse of trees and stopped.

"There's a bird here, Dad," she said quietly. I took a deep breath, then one step. A second step. A third, and the grouse blew up over my shoulder. I took it going away with the first tube.

Ghost was on it, nuzzling and softly mouthing the warm body. She was deliriously happy. So was I. All I could do was hug her neck, rub her all over and laugh. The fan measured 13 inches, tip-to-tip. Still our biggest ever.

"Okay," I finally said, smoothing everyone's ruffled feathers. "Let's go home and show Mom our bird."

Chapter 8

No Wonder the Dogs Sometimes Run Away

I was seven or eight—I don't remember exactly—when I Did It for the first time. Ran away from home, I mean.

Probably it was because of some cataclysmic event in my life like not being allowed to jump off the roof and fly like Superman.

Or because I didn't get a pony for Christmas (although I got darned near everything else—including a coonskin cap—that Strauss' toy department inventoried that year).

Maybe I just had a bad case of wanderlust.

All I remember is tying a pillowcase to a stick like I had seen Mickey Mouse—I think—do in a cartoon. It was filled with my Life Essentials. Things like Oreos, a few marbles, and my favorite baseball cards. I hadn't thought to slap together a ham sandwich.

I wasn't worried about water. Back then you could get a mouthful out of anybody's garden hose with no complaints. It simply was what kids *did*. Heck, you could even pound on the door and they'd bring you a glass!

I'd only walked a couple of blocks when I ran into Johnny Rosenberger. "Hey," he said, "watcha got in the bag?"

"Some stuff," I replied diffidently. "Why?"

"I dunno. Just looks funny. That's all."

"What's funny about runnin' away?" I said, sticking out my chin confidently because Johnny was a lot smaller than me and I knew I could knock him down and scram. Except he was a good kid and I didn't want to knock him down.

He cocked his head, looked puzzled, and sat on the grass. So, I sat on the grass too.

"Why ya' runnin away? Bust a lamp or somethin'?"

We looked at each other for eternity. In other words, the time it takes to get from first grade into second. And I couldn't come up with one ding-dong reason for running away.

"Aww, I was only kiddin'," I finally said. "Wanna shoot some marbles?"

I'll never know for sure, of course, but Ghost might have felt the same way I had. We both were, relatively speaking, about the same age when she took off for the first time.

Of course, if truth be told, I have a hunch she really ran away out of embarrassment because she finally figured out what a lousy shot I was.

I never kept a diary when I was growing up. It's just not the sort of thing a guy does. But I understand, now that I keep a log-book chronicling all of our hunts, why a diary is private. There are lots of things in there you wouldn't want anyone else to read. Ever.

Take October 26, 1997, for instance. What I recorded is embarrassing, really, but I suppose psychoanalysts among you probably will say that confessing is somehow therapeutic.

Personally, I think that might be bullshit, but I'll own up nevertheless.

"Ghost started coming of age at just 23 weeks old," I wrote. "Ben pointed a woodcock and Ghost stopped sniffing around in the leaves off to my left, ran over and backed his point. John Norcross and I both missed the bird.

"A few minutes later, Ben pointed a grouse. Ghost backed him, and I missed that one, too. The Colonel later claimed he never saw the bird, but I distinctly remember his Browning booming. Twice.

"Just before we reached the old logging road that led back to my truck, Ghost went on point. I moved in close and a grouse zipped up through the bare popple branches, straightened out and flew away while I was fumbling with the safety catch."

Ghost didn't know enough at the time to be disgusted with my inept performance. A week later, when I didn't pull the trigger on two grouse she had worked long and hard to pin, she still looked at me with a merely puzzled expression.

Finally, she'd had enough.

We were hunting down along the South Branch of the Au Sable River, in the 1,500-acre tract of trout and grouse heaven that George Mason gave to the state of Michigan more than 50 years ago.

He was president of American Motors and Nash-Kelvinator at the time, and carried a lot of weight. Physically and metaphorically. So, he persuaded several of his auto-making pals to "sell" him their river frontage for a buck each. More than a thousand feet of frontage by maybe 150 feet deep! On both sides of the river.

When he died in 1954—after planting the seed of what ultimately would germinate into Trout Unlimited—his will deeded all that acreage to the state as a fishing and hunting preserve open to the public. There's even a rustic chapel there, where sometimes people get married, or swear their love. Or maybe swear at their dogs.

I'd fished for big trout around Daisy Bend, just downstream, plenty of times but never had hunted the area. "My boy," Norcross told me as we were driving in, "it's a gem. A real gem."

So, here we were. Ghost was locked up and the grouse, an experienced old bird, took off low. Almost skimming the tops of the weeds. I couldn't shoot without hitting Ghost.

Without even looking to find out why I didn't pull the trigger, Ghost whipped to her right and pointed another grouse. This one was no dummy, either. It dodged behind a big pine tree and disappeared like Houdini. When I didn't shoot—again—Ghost finally turned and stared at me.

She sorta cocked her head, then more or less asked me "What's up buster? You told me to find the birds, and I DID! When are you going to throw in and do your part?"

I just shrugged. And I guess I looked sorta sheepish.

She turned away, trotted off, and went swimming. I couldn't really find fault with her. I pretty much felt like doing the same thing. Maybe another "baptism" would cleanse me of such poor shooting.

But I do I remember thinking at the time that she was getting a bit uppity for such a young dog.

Then I dropped a couple of woodcock and a grouse during the next few hunts and had pretty much worked my way back into Ghost's good graces.

We were feeling especially friendly toward each other the morning Ghost pointed five woodcock and two grouse, practically in our front yard. I was typically inept on the grouse, but Bill McKellar, my closest neighbor, and I got four of the woodcock.

We coulda/shoulda had a fifth.

All of us were tired and a couple of us had too many beers the night before. I won't incriminate anyone in particular, though. So I was walking Ghost home on the leash when she stopped a couple of hundred yards from our house.

Bill and I looked at each other like *"Riiight!"* I hadn't learned yet that when Ghost goes on point she's *never* kidding. I had my hands full of leash, of course, and Bill had an unloaded 20 bore slung over his shoulder when that woodcock flew off.

Fortunately, Ghost was pretty tired by then so she calmly watched it corkscrew through the popples and just trotted home, still spitting feathers out of her mouth. Maybe she was just being nice to Bill.

Sometimes she's considerate that way.

One frozen moment in time gave the Colonel enough memories to carry him through a "lost" hunting season.

Chapter 9

Sometimes Time Does Stand Still

The Colonel was having a particularly cranky morning, huffing and grumping even before the front door slammed shut behind him.

"Watchoutformylawn, dammit!" he yelped, as my pickup truck crunched over the dead oak leaves in the middle of his driveway. "Whereinhell'dya learn to drive that thing? Some ox path in Italy?"

Since I was accustomed to his tirades, I just smiled and dropped the tailgate so Ben, who'd raced around the house from the back yard, could do his ritual "Fosbury Flop" into the bed of my truck.

"Hiya, schweetheart," Ben cooed to Ghost in his best Bogey imitation. She, in turn, merely curled her lip and snuggled deeper into the soft pillow inside her crate.

"Humph," Ben snorted. "I've been in better joints than this. And with better dames than YOU." Actually, he was lying about that last part and everybody knew it. But, when he shuffled around a few towels and thumped down into a circle of setter, I noticed he was keeping his distance from Ghost.

"Smart boy," I thought. Come to think of it, Kate had been a bit grumpy at breakfast, too. But then, she's *always* that way until two or three mugs of bitter-strong coffee get her blood veins pumped up big and blue.

I finally tuned in the Colonel, who was shoving his shotgun case, orange vest, and a hamper of sandwiches into a corner where Ben couldn't reach, but I still couldn't figure out what had him wound so tightly.

"Coffee?" I asked politely.

"No."

"Tea?"

"No, dammit!"

"Me?" I said, coyly parroting an old United Airlines joke and batting my eyelashes. *That* finally got him laughing.

"Let's get going," he said, trying to be gruff and ready.

"Not so fast, hotshot. I wanna know why you're in such a snit. Are you mad at me for something?" I asked.

John Norcross looked at me with misery plastered across his white-stubbled face. "Aw, we're going to France," he said, grimacing.

"When?"

"Next Tuesday."

"No way," I replied. "I still have preseason orders to wrap up! [This happened way back when I was a sales rep in the fly tackle industry] Besides, trout season's closed over there, and I'd rather shoot grouse than driven pheasant anytime."

"Not *you*, dammit! I am going to France. With *Jacqueline*. To visit her family for six weeks." *Jacqueline*, of course, being the *Mrs*. John Norcross.

I was stunned.

"SIX WEEKS!?! Hell, that'll wipe out the rest of bird season. You can't just run off to Paris…"

"Toulon!" he interrupted.

"…wherever! Are you *nuts*? You can't fly off to France *now*."

The Colonel stared at me balefully. "My boy, how long have you been married?"

I did the quick arithmetic, shrugged, and nodded sadly.

"Yeah, you're right. Why is it wives win every time?"

John gave me a withering look and clumsily hoisted himself into my truck without another word.

We both were quiet while I drove.

When the truck hit a pothole in the sandy ox path I'd been negotiating, it jarred the truck so hard a couple of lug nuts must have spun loose from the right front wheel. John seemed to come out of a coma. "Dammit! Exactly where in hell are you going?"

"Deward. Thought we'd check out a few thickets that Kate and I walk through when we fish that stretch downstream from the old mill. Always looked birdy. To men, anyway. You can decide." *You always do,* I thought to myself.

Several chokecherry trees had blown down since Kate and I had been there near the end of trout season. Which meant I had to stop the truck, climb out, and armwrestle them off the narrow two-track.

"Um, I would not be averse to getting a little help with these," I told The Colonel as I eased a splinter from the underside of my left thumb. "I mean, I really wouldn't want to hog all the fun. Yaknow?"

Norcross more or less looked down his nose at me and was quiet for several heartbeats.

"At my age, I do the ordering, m'boy, not the work. And you'd best move a bit more quickly. It'll soon be too hot for the dogs to have good scenting wind."

No. I won't tell you what went through my mind at that particular instant. What I finally did say — after biting a big chunk out of my tongue — was, "I already know how to break kindling, Oh Exalted Master. I really don't need the practice."

A half-mile and two more deadfalls later I tucked the truck under the shade of three pine trees and reached for a water jug.

"Water the dogs first," Norcross said. "Dammit! Don't you remember *anything* I've told you after all the times we've hunted together?

"You take care of the dogs first, your shotgun second and Yourself last. Don't ever forget that again." I didn't forget it *this time,* I thought — but kept quiet anyway.

As soon as I dropped the tailgate, Ben stamped out his cigarette, glanced contemptuously at Ghost, and went off to investigate a couple of nearby bushes. The Colonel thought about that for a moment, then ambled off to do the same.

Ghost, being a lady on rare occasions, decided that a long drink of cold water would be a very good thing before *she* went in search of a suitable spot for "personal relief."

She wasn't fooling me one bit, though. I snapped a long leash to her collar before lifting her down from the truck (I know, I know — but she was a lot smaller than Ben) because sure as hell she'd have been gone looking for birds in the blink of an eye.

Even though she was still a kid, I'd seen her, uh, "dribble" her way onto point if she picked up the merest whiff of a bird. In fact, the number of times she "locked up" while leashed — and we subsequently shot (or missed) a bird — is legendary.

I was lifting Ghost back into her crate — Ben, being senior in rank, always rated the first covert — when The Colonel quietly told me to "wire her up." I gave him a quick glance, didn't say anything, and rummaged through the gear bag.

Finally, with beepers and zappers strapped onto both dogs, bells tinkling, and pockets bulging with 20-bore hulls, we went off in search of grouse.

Ben was at heel. Ghost was straining at her leash. John looked disdainfully from her to me and shook his head. "When," he asked, "are you going to properly train that dog?"

Frankly, I didn't have much of an excuse, so I just shut up.

Cutting north off the old logging road, I unleashed Ghost and we slogged through a small blackberry patch, skidded to the bottom of a shallow ravine, and jumped a small bog of stinkweed. There was a stand of popples on the opposite crest, and their leaves were just beginning to show a faint golden color through the sunlight.

It was a pretty sight, and I was about to mention that to John when I heard "Beeeep. Beeeep. Beeeep," and looked to my left. John, whose hearing had been deteriorating rapidly, was oblivious to Ben's point. Ghost—off to my right—stared at Ben, then raised her eyebrows at me.

I nodded at her once. She glided past me and then John, lithe as a panther stalking a calf. Thirty feet from Ben, who was trembling ever-so-slightly, she stopped and stared straight ahead. Her tail went rigid. She never moved.

Time more or less stood still while I watched the dogs. Nero fiddled and Romeo burned. Cleopatra entreated Antony for a backrub. Or something. Finally, I impatiently asked The Colonel "You gonna shoot that bird?"

John appeared puzzled, then realized Ghost was honoring Ben's point. He smiled. "*Surprised*," I thought. But he didn't move to kick up the bird. He just stood there, looking at them so long that I thought I heard a chunk of the Coliseum's façade fall off.

Ben whined. Just a little bit. Ghost cut her eyes sideways to ask me "what the heck's going on here?" I stood where I was. This wasn't my play.

When the grouse "whirrrrr"-ed away both dogs deflated like punctured balloons. Ben decided to scratch his right ear. Ghost looked at me accusingly.

John sighed and started walking. Not angrily, mind you. Just walking. Through the brush and around the blowdowns, with just a hint of a smile on his seamed face.

Ghost sidled up to Ben and bumped his right side. Just a little bit. Then they took off in separate directions, testing the limits before a whistle from me—or a tingle in Ben's collar—brought them closer.

We threaded through some young popples that had been chewed down by beavers, and came out of the brush alongside the Manistee River. The dogs found a low spot where they could drink its 50-degree water and soak their hot paws.

"Take my shotgun," John said. "I need to sit down. That big log up there looks like God made it into a bench just for me. Did you remember to bring some water?"

I pocketed the hulls from both Brownings and propped them firmly in the crotches of a small white pine. Pulling two bottles out of my vest, I handed him the one labeled JOHN and looked for a place to sit while he took a long pull.

After hanging my game vest on a dead branch, I slid down into a sitting position with my back against the tree. I could see small mayflies dancing above the river in the brilliant sunlight. A trout was rising upstream in the fast water alongside a log.

The fingernails-on-chalkboard squawk of a great blue heron finally broke the quiet, and I noticed Ben and Ghost were rooting around an ancient, rotted stump—probably where a black bear had been looking for beetles to eat.

When a large shadow passed over them, I looked up.

"Eagle," I said to John, pointing.

"The Indians claim it's good luck when an eagle circles you," John said without hesitation. "They say it's a sign that God is watching over you. That you're blessed."

I was still thinking about that when Ghost, who'd been wiggling around, scratching her back on the soft grass, rolled down the gentle slope, and "splooshed!" into the river.

She came up from underneath the water, indignantly blowing and snorting, then swam back upstream. Scrambling up the crumbling bank, she shook all over from her white-capped left ear to the tip of her magnificently feathered tail.

The trout quit rising. Ben looked startled and hid behind a tree, peeking at her curiously. John broke into a grin, then started to guffaw.

"Shhhhh!" I whispered to him. "Don't laugh or it'll hurt her feelings."

He looked at me sorta strangely for a second, then nodded and took another long drink of water.

Ben sniffed at Ghost tentatively, then backed off when she flopped down—farther away from the river this time, I noted—and started rolling in the dry grass.

The trout fed again. The eagle flew off. John flipped the empty water bottle to me. "This has been a good day," he finally said. "It will carry me through six agonizing weeks.

"Let's go home, m'boy."

Paybacks can be awfully nice sometimes, such as the friendship that developed between me and Mike Beatty, and Ghost and Sadie.

Chapter 10

What Goes Around Really Comes Around

Thirty-five years ago, before I learned the true meaning of life, I actually thought October mornings had been created so I could stand waist-deep in a swiftly flowing river and chunk flies at some stupid fish.

On this bleak break of dawn I'd been awake since two, probably with about that many hours' sleep; driven in an eerie fog—praying I wouldn't smack a deer—for three; schlepped through black, gooey riverbank muck for the better part of yet another hour.

What a moron.

All so that I could spend eight hours freezing my ass off in 40-degree water trying to irritate some 30-pound salmon, that already was on the verge of death, into eating an artificial fly.

To top it off, these Chinook—I also ultimately learned—were only interested in one thing. Sex. And not with me.

The only consolation, if you wanna be charitable and call it that, is that this particular occasion was a social gathering of the Red Cedar Fly Fishers. It's a chapter of the Federation of Fly Fishers, and a bunch of us were on a weekend expedition to the Pere Marquette River in northwest Michigan.

A few of the guys, like Jim Schramm, Pete Barnes, and Terry Lyons, were veterans at this game. I was third-string maybe working toward second-team status. Which meant I'd done this before.

You might know an old doctor joke. It goes "In medical school you watch a surgical procedure Week One. You perform it Week Two. You teach it Week Three."

I was in Week Three.

My two hands-on students, so to speak, were Tom Little and Mike Beatty. They were members of the RCFF, but this salmon fishing thing was a mystery to them. *Salmo Virginius*, so to speak.

They weren't really "mine," you understand. But they were so totally bewildered by the leaders, tippets, knots, flies and—hell, everything—that I just took them into protective custody.

Mike hooked a salmon that day. I don't remember if he landed it. Probably not. But he remembered. Oh, did he ever remember.

The club used to meet in Okemos, a high-class suburb of Michigan State University. On Tuesday evenings, as I recall. I was talking with a couple of guys the week after our "outing" when Mike walked in. He waited till I was alone, then sidled over.

"You do any bird hunting?" he asked, sorta tentatively. "Pheasant, I mean."

"No, but I'd like to," I confessed. "I don't have a hunting dog, or access to good pheasant cover. But I remember how much my buddy's grandpa loved it when I was a kid growing up in Ohio."

"Maybe," he said, "you'd like to come out to my farm. It's between St. John's and Laingsburg, and we've got a really nice population of wild pheasant.

"The season opens next week. On the twentieth. Can you come on the twenty-second or twenty-third? I already made plans for the opener."

This was back in the early 90s, when my little terrier CJ was big on grouse but short on legs. There was absolutely no way she'd ever bust through the thick switchgrass, bluestem and sorghum that pheasant so adore.

Besides, a tough old rooster might have beat her to death.

"Um, would it be alright if I brought my uncle along? He has an English setter." Mike was between dogs at the time, and said that would be fine.

Booshie, the first Llewellyn I ever hunted over, was a big tall boy with lots of enthusiasm and a decent nose. He did his part that day, but we didn't.

It was, however, the beginning of a deep friendship with Mike, and we began hunting pheasant for at least a day or two every year.

A couple of months after I got Ghost, Mike got Sadie, another English setter, and our time together following dogs in the woods increased exponentially.

We trade off. He comes up to sit on the porch in Deward and listen to the nightingales sing in June. If we get inspired enough, sometimes we even do a little trout fishing. I go to Laingsburg for the pheasant opener between our grouse hunts, then park myself in front of his fireplace the night before deer opener.

It was during one of Mike's trips north for grouse that Sadie came within a few minutes of dying.

We hadn't been in the woods very long. It was hot and we were sweating already. Mike was following Sadie and I was off looking for Ghost. I could hear Mike call and call and call again, each time with a bit more impatience at her impertinence.

Mike was quiet for a while, then I was shocked by his yell.

"TONY! Come quick. It's Sadie! I need help!"

Luck was with me right then. Ghost had just come nosing around for a drink of water, so I snapped on her leash, fastened it to a small tree, and crashed through the brush to the sound of Mike's frantic calls.

Sadie was covered with blood.

"A stick punctured the inside of her leg," he said. "It won't stop bleeding!"

I found out a long time ago that military-style web belts (one-size-fits-all) come in mighty handy when you're fooling around in the outdoors. They shore up tent posts or hang an improvised shower bag. Wrap one around a tree, twist your barrel through it once, and it's better than a sling for holding a rifle steady. You can even use one to make a dog leash or muzzle.

This day, mine made a tourniquet.

Shoving a pair of my gloves against the spurting blood, I pulled the belt tight and told Mike to carry her to the road. I'd get the truck.

"I can't carry her and keep it from bleeding," Mike said.

"Open your mouth," I told him, cinched the belt tighter, and shoved the end of it between his teeth. "Pull hard and let's get going."

We were only a few miles from Paul Mesack's vet clinic, so I called to give them a heads-up, turned on my emergency flashers and figured a speeding ticket was worth Sadie's life.

Mike was a wreck that night. I understood completely, and poured each of us a couple extra fingers of bourbon. Neither of us slept very well. Even Ghost was restless.

"It was a close call," Paul told us the next morning. "The left femoral vein had a big hole in it. She nearly bled out, but she'll be alright. She's done hunting for a few weeks, though."

I took Ghost and Ben down for the pheasant opener two weeks later and have to say that Sadie didn't miss a thing. Pheasant were scarce. In fact, despite Mike's plantings and protection, the situation deteriorated to the point that we've left the roosters alone the past few seasons.

"The cornfields are absolutely black with turkey, but I haven't even heard a rooster cackle," Mike sadly said as last October's opener neared. "No matter what I do, we just aren't seeing the birds (pheasant) like we used to."

In their place, Mike has substituted quail and added a setter pup named Belle, who thinks those little speckled birds are wonderful fun. So does Ghost.

We were sitting by the fire one evening last season. Sadie was on Mike's lap, and Belle was snoring on the sofa. Ghost was on the floor next to me.

"Ya know," Mike said after staring into the fire for a while, "when you gave up your day of fishing on the Pere Marquette to teach me about salmon, all those years ago, I didn't think I was ever going to be able to repay that kindness."

He smiled. So did I, and raised my glass in salute. Ghost started to softly snore, content to be warm and cozy with Dad after another wonderful day of hunting. It's so nice to be with good friends.

Nothing ever diminished Ghost's desire to find birds.

Chapter 11

Sheep, Pheasant, and Near-Death

It's funny how dogs will surprise you sometimes. Like when Ghost was about four.

We were on our way to hunt pheasant in Montana and Ghost politely informed me that I should pull off to the side of the road so that she could, well…you know.

She hopped out of the truck and naturally started investigating the environment. A flock of sheep on the other side of the fence started "baaaaaaing" and running toward us, kicking at each other like groupies at a rock concert.

Meanwhile, Ghost was nosing around in four inches of snow that wasn't supposed to be on the ground yet. Sorta snuffling, and scraping it around so that she wouldn't freeze her delicate, well, you know…and then all those sheep had somehow pressed up against the fence, screaming for autographs or something.

Ghost was regally oblivious until the proverbial black sheep in the flock shouldered through the madding crowd and planted itself next to the fence. Opposite Ghost. Staring intently.

Now, on other occasions when she wasn't happy I've heard Ghost bark like a drill instructor dressing down a terrified grunt who was unbuttoned, had scuffed boots, or God forbid, was holding a filthy weapon.

So I was plumb dumbfounded when she never said a word to that Big Black Sheep.

Nope. She just stood up straight and tall. Real rigid-like, with her knees locked tight. Then she squinted her eyes like ole

Clint Eastwood woulda done in a big-money Texas Hold-Em, and did a Don King thingy with the hair on the back of her neck.

Her upper lip curled high and her lower jaw dropped down and I'll be danged if old Lon Chaney wouldn't have wept in joy at finding Dracula's Dog right there on the edge of Montana Highway 200.

About that time all those sheep stopped stomping and clapping and whistling for lunch. What they did was to take a few real slow steps backward. Then a few more.

Actually, they sorta fanned out off to each side like you see in those old western movies. You know, when there's gonna be a gunfight in the middle of Main Street and the citizens don't want to get any of *that* on themselves.

And just like that Blackie was all alone, eyeball to eyeball with Dracula's Dog, who by now had a stringy glob of drool hanging from her lower jaw. Long, sharp, white teeth glinted like icicles in the November sun.

Now, I was a sportswriter for a lot of years and I watched Mercury Morris live up to his name. Bobby Orr was a blur going down the ice even on only one good leg. And nobody was fasterer than King Richard when he busted loose and left those ole moonshiners wondering whereinhell that boy got to.

But let me tell you none of them held a *candle* to that Baa Baa Blacksheep when it *vaporized* toward Someplace Else Montana.

Ghost licked her lips, winked at me conspiratorially, squatted for a nanosecond, then told me it was time to hie on toward camp so we could rustle up some grub and catch a good night's sleep before showing these Montana pheasants a thing or two.

I found Skip's ranch a bit north of Great Falls, someplace around Vaughn, without too much trouble. Then we headed back toward town for a license and some of the basic food groups. Things like bread and cold beer.

I was frying sausage and heating spaghetti sauce when Gospo pulled in trailing his future brother-in-law, Mark, and a big blockheaded Gordon setter named Rye, who immediately fell in love with Ghost.

"Oh, Dad—she's so *pretty*," Rye wailed. Alas, his lust went unrequited and they promptly had a non-lover's spat over the food dish. Afterward, Ghost haughtily strode to my sleeping bag, did the obligatory three-times-in-a-circle, and fell asleep. Rye huffed a couple of times and flopped down under the table at Gospo's feet.

It was overcast the next morning when Ghost almost died.

We'd only been hunting a half hour, but Ghost has two speeds: Off and Firewall. As a result, she heats up pretty fast, and likes to jump into any available water source. Which, in this case, was Muddy Creek. Except it was partially frozen over in the middle, with shelf ice along each bank.

So when she blithely trotted through the snow and slid into the water, it came as a puzzling surprise to her when she couldn't simply climb out on the other side and keep on hunting.

One glance at the big patches of ice in mid-stream turned my blood as cold as that water. I yelled "Right here!" and Ghost paddled back to the near bank with a curious expression on her face. Of course, she couldn't pull herself up onto the ice on this side, either.

I immediately set down my Beretta, stretched out flat on the ice, grabbed her collar, and gave a serious yank.

She flopped and shook like a beached trout. Then I'll be danged if she didn't flip me that big grin with her tongue lolling out the side of her mouth and yell "that was GREAT Dad, now let's go find those birds!" Which is precisely what she did.

It was in one of those football-shaped thickets about the size of your average living room where she once and forever made believers out of John Gospodarek and Mark Johnson.

Rye was off looking for birds somewhere around Billings, but Ghost stuck her nose into that patch of shrubs and wispy little trees and announced that we'd best get ready.

Mark went over to the far side, and I walked into the middle. "I'll handle the flush, and you guys take the birds," I said, and asked Ghost if she'd mind showing me exactly where they were.

She looked up rather crossly, I thought, and just poked her chin higher into the air. "Okay," I told her, "be like that." At which point she twitched her nose a couple of times and took a couple of very slow steps deeper into the thicket.

We got almost to the end before there was a flurry of wings, but no gunshots, when three hens took off like teenagers who just got caught stealing hubcaps. Ghost looked at each of us in turn and shook her head in disgust.

Then she turned around and locked up on point again. So, I yelled to the guys and started kicking the clumps of snowy switchgrass. I kicked. And I kicked. I kicked some more.

Finally, I told Ghost to knock it off because she was pointing old scent from those hens. She sorta spat out a mouthful of snow and something I couldn't quite hear. When I told her "Let's go find some birds" she glared back and rather rudely told me she already HAD found a bird and that it was right here.

Being a boy of little faith at that moment, I impatiently reached down and grabbed her collar. "NoNoNo!" she screamed. I pulled her away even as she was digging all four paws into the snow. Ghost finally gave up and trotted off, but she wasn't happy about it.

An hour later we were on our way back to the bunkhouse. As we neared Three Hen Thicket, Ghost glanced at me and nodded her head in that direction. "Will you *please* come on over here and shoot that bird?" she said, and promptly locked on point in exactly the spot where I'd dragged her away.

I looked at John. He looked at Mark. Mark looked at Ghost—who was by now quivering like a feathery statue—then took three steps forward and stepped on a rooster that thundered out of those weeds like the Cannonball Express.

All three of us stared as it flew away. Then we looked at Ghost, who reached up with her right hind foot and nonchalantly scratched a cocklebur from her ear with an "I told you so" expression on her face.

From then on, every time Ghost went on point John would say "I believe her." Time after time roosters would cackle. Usually, it was their last cackle.

The following morning brought a brilliant blue sky. Sunlight sparkled off six inches of snow. The temperature hovered at four degrees and the feathering on Ghost's legs and tail was frozen solid.

It didn't seem to matter, though. We worked along the draws, and up over the rises where the barley stubble attracted those pheasants by the hundreds, especially about three in the afternoon.

Of course you couldn't walk within shooting distance of those wide-open birds, but it was fun to sit in the truck and marvel at how many there were.

The best hunting was down in the draws, and in the thick stuff alongside Muddy Creek. So we hunted those hard for two days and filled our legal limits and ate and drank and laughed.

Not once, though, did Ghost decide to take another plunge into that icy water. I even asked her if she wanted to go swimming.

I didn't quite catch her response. But I don't think it was very nice.

Chapter 12

Yogi Said "Ya Shudda Stood In Bed!"

I was making my "Western Swing" over to Wisconsin and Minnesota. This was during my days as a manufacturer's rep in the fly fishing business, and it was preseason order time.

It also was getting pretty damned close to the end of grouse season. So, keeping my priorities in perspective, I used Steve Sendek's cabin on the Michigan-Wisconsin border as a place to fall asleep when I wasn't casting fly rods with shop owners or chasing Ghost around northern Wisconsin or the Uper Peninsula.

The business portion of my trip worked out pretty well, I guess. The rod company had brought out some sweet new models, and so did the fly line people I worked for. My portable fax machine stayed busy every evening and my bosses were happy.

I, on the other hand, was miserable.

Paul Mesack and his buddy Bruce Patrick, a retired fish cop, came up from Grayling to hunt with us. Steve's hand-hewn log cabin has plenty of bunks, so that wasn't an issue.

Dogs? Sure, I had Ghost. Paul brought his new French Brittany, Shadow, and Steve had a couple of his German shorthairs, Quinta and D (appropriately short for Demon).

Birds? Plenty, as usual, up here where the bears and wolves outnumber us humans and dogs on any given day. Or night.

Opportunities? Well, now there's the crux of the problem. Which, I regretfully have to admit, was me. I couldn't hit a bull in the butt with a bass fiddle.

Ghost and I pulled into town around noon on Wednesday, November 1, amid heavy wind and rain showers. "Charming," I thought. "Simply charming."

When I stopped at Angelli's Market for a few camp goodies I called Kate on my spiffy new "bag" phone. She said it was balmy with a brilliant blue sky in Deward. Charming. We drove on to Steve's camp, settled in for the night and hoped for the best.

Dawn broke way too early and I could hear tree limbs groaning in the wind. I groaned, too, and told Ghost to go back to sleep. She didn't need a whole lot more encouragement, and snuffled deeper into the folds of my sleeping bag.

The woodburner wasn't, and there was a definite chill in the air. I burrowed into the covers pretty well, too, and rolled closer to Ghost.

When Joe Schober's old truck finally clattered down the nasty sand-and-rock two-track that ends at Steve's camp, I shivered into a shirt and my hunting pants. It was time to mess with bacon and eggs.

Over breakfast, I listened to Steve and Joe jawbone about all the guys and girls they'd grown up with in Iron River. Most of them still lived there. In fact, hardly any of Steve's friends or family could figure out what had possessed him to abandon God's Country.

"Hell, he went all the way Down Below [meaning south of the Mackinac Bridge] to college," his cousin, Bob, whispered to me once, incredulously. "Now he works with the damned fish cops! (meaning the Department of Natural Resources and Environment).

"He always was a bit 'different'. But, hell, he's family so whaddaya gonna do?"

It was 10:30 before we finally took our shotguns down from the pegs, belching and...you know. Ghost and Quinta bashed into each other getting out the door then sniffed at each other's, well...as dogs will do.

When they took off toward the swamp I followed Ghost. Steve went with Quinta. Joe had the good sense to sit on a log and wait to see who went on point first.

Turned out it was Ghost. Joe finally ambled up and missed that bird, a pretty easy High House Two. We slogged through the black muck, deeper into the cedars, where Ghost made a really classy point after crawling under a big, rotten deadfall. I missed with both tubes.

At the edge of a weedy clearing, with a little trickle of a creek on one side and dense cedars on the other, Ghost locked tight. This obviously was a young grouse that suffered from very poor "situational awareness" because it flew straight across the wide open spaces.

I missed again.

Ghost didn't say anything. Just sighed heavily and stalked off on very stiff legs. She was a bit miffed.

By the time we got back to the cabin Ghost had made six points and never got a single feather in her mouth. Steve, on the other hand, had shot two grouse over Quinta. Ghost was mortified by my shooting. She wouldn't even look at me.

Paul and Bruce pulled in shortly after we started warming chili, and venison stew, for lunch. Ghost was pouting. Quinta was still hacking up feathers. I studied the little squirt of a dog Paul had brought, but didn't say anything. Steve sorta stifled a laugh. Joe coulda been a cigar store Indian.

"I know, I know," Paul said, abashed. He should, after all, KNOW better about such things. "Judy wanted him," Paul mumbled, trying real hard to lay the blame on his wife. The rest of us just looked at each other. We weren't buying it.

"Dog's a bit on the puny side, dontcha think?" was all that Joe finally said. Steve and I kept quiet. After all, there really wasn't much more to add after that.

Well, we poked around out there for the next few days watching the dogs have fun. The birds were skittish, and our shooting, mostly, was abysmal. Steve got another bird, Bruce shot one, and Paul knocked down two. Me? I don't even want to go there!

On the afternoon of our final hunt, before everybody shook loose for home, we were down by the big old barn that Steve's great-grandfather built about a hundred years ago.

Parked inside is a really ancient tractor that looks nearly new. "Been there as long as I can remember," Steve said with a shrug. Over in the weeds there are a couple of flatbed trucks that Capone might have used when he ran Chicago. And a bunch of worn out cars. Two of them, I noticed, were Edsels.

I was going to ask Steve about all of that rusting steel, but a grouse got up just about then and I took a shot at it and missed and Ghost got mad and ran off. Again.

About seven hours later, Orion's belt was dangling in the night sky when I coasted to a stop by the kitchen door. The house was all lit up, and I could see Kate through the big windows. She turned and waved, an oversize oven mitt on each hand.

"Thought you might like some warm chocolate chip cookies," she said, stuffing one into my mouth. Ghost got an Alpo Liver Snap and was equally happy. "How'd the hunt go?"

"Never got a grouse," I said. Ghost sorta coughed.

"Humph. I got one today," Kate said.

I stared. "You wanna tell me about that?" Kate doesn't hunt anything but brook trout, and she never kills those, either.

"Well, there's been one eating the chokecherries on that tree the past few days." She pointed behind us. "This afternoon, I looked out the kitchen door and he was right here at the foot of the steps. Standing on Ghost's long lead."

"Whattadya do, swat him with a broom?" I said.

"Nah. He flew back into the tree and ate more of those chokecherries. A lot of them, actually. And I guess they were fermented because he started acting kinda woozy. Like he was drunk or something.

"Then he took off and flew right into my bathroom window. Which was closed, of course. Silly thing broke its neck. We're having him for dinner tonight."

The phrase "Play Like a Champion Today" was never more appropriate than it was whenever Ghost was in the field.

CHAPTER 13

COMING OF AGE LIKE A CHAMPION

Every bird dog, if it's worth being called a bird dog, ultimately reaches a very special moment in time. It has an epiphany—if that doesn't sound too awfully blasphemous to you—when the light bulb clicks on in full brilliance and he or she understands what life is about.

Meaning birds.

Sad to say, some wannabes with fancy names and a snotty lineage never cut the mustard. You've seen 'em. Usually they tail around after some guy wearing a herringbone jacket with suede patches on the elbows, a Ruark safari hat, and thousand-dollar Wellingtons.

Sure. He stinks up the gun club with obnoxious pipe tobacco while he talks through his teeth in that infuriating nasally way about his Italian doubles (which the rest of us would *kill* for, truth be told) and the big-money shoots he's won down in Texas, where folks like Pickens and Lawrence and Austin hang their Purdeys and Greeners.

But he's just another Flim-Flam Man. Hardly a nine-shot of truth in anything he says, and it's too damned bad that he ruined what might have turned out to be a pretty good gun dog.

The poor thing's usually a black or chocolate lab that lives in a spotless kennel with a cushy bed and fenced-in enclosure 360 days a year. It never ate the innards from a dead 'possum or flopped flat and drank out of a mud puddle. Or ran off to the next county looking for romance. Like *some* dogs I could name.

Well, I've sorta "gone to Abilene," as Kate is wont to accuse me of doing, but now I'm about ready to tell you all the details of Ghost's magic moment.

At Notre Dame, when the football team clatters down the steps from its second-floor locker room, headed to the field on those beautiful October afternoons, there's a tight little landing with a ninety-degree turn to the left.

High on that wall, painted large in blue and gold is a sign that every man whaps his hand against on the way out to do battle. It reads "Play Like A Champion Today."

Some do, some don't.

I guess that's the way life is for dogs as well as men. Some simply never get the chance. Some fail shamefully. Some—but only a very few—really do have "the right stuff" to become Champions.

Ghost is one of those Champions.

I told you already about her first retrieve, and how JD Korte wanted to pay me forty-five-hundred bucks to own her. And her first grouse point in front of the tree where our ashes will be scattered, and her Montana pheasant near-death experience in Muddy Creek.

But quite obviously the defining moment, when I knew that I had lucked into somebody really special, was the day I marked my logbook with five stars and the bold headline GHOST'S BEST DAY EVER!!

Here's how it happened.

Marc Norcross met me that morning at the Grayling High School parking lot. This was a while ago, when nobody ran you off or called the sheriff because you had a shotgun on school property. Even in northern Michigan, where kids practically pop from the womb holding a gun, they're getting picky about that stuff these days.

Anyway, it was sunny and about 65 degrees with no wind when Marc showed up. Ben stuck his head out the window to say hello—one setter to another—and we all drove off to the humid hunting grounds.

It was late September, and there still were a lot of leaves on the trees, but I was feeling really good about our prospects until I saw Marc pull a goofy little gun out of its case. With a goofy little grin on his face. I could tell already that he knew better. His dad would have hided him.

"The latest acquisition for my collection," he said, proudly. "I sneaked it into the house and Anne doesn't even know I bought it."

Well now. The first thought that ran through my mind was *why in hell would you WANT to buy something like that?* What I *said* was "Uh, Marc, why in hell would you WANT to buy something like that?"

You see, "that" was a 12-bore double with 19-inch barrels. The sort of weapon a friend of mine who worked for the Alcohol Tobacco & Firearms division of the federal government once called "a street sweeper."

It's a great little weapon in a gang war, but of extremely dubious value for killing anything—or anybody—beyond 20 feet away. Which Marc learned pretty quickly.

So we get out into the woods. Ben runs off to the left and Ghost is poking around in the crunchy leaves someplace. I didn't really know exactly where, to tell you the truth. Then I heard her beeper do its thing and headed off in that direction.

Marc and Ben both wandered over and when the woodcock went up it was in Marc's face. Sure, he was as surprised as Ben that the bird was practically underneath his right boot. Feathers in your face can be disconcerting. So, I guess maybe he did have a reasonable excuse for what happened next.

He missed. Badly. Humiliatingly badly.

Now, you need to remember that this is Colonel John Norcross' son. Neither one ever took lightly missing a shot on grouse or woodcock in all the days we went afield. I mean, *ever*. For the first year under The Colonel's tutelage I thought "Dammit!" was my new nickname.

So, I decided to keep my mouth clamped firmly shut as we all watched that woodcock twitter away. Ben glanced at me, then made serious eye contact with Ghost. She sorta shrugged and trotted off, with Ben in her wake. I kept quiet. Marc seethed.

That was bad. It got worse. By the end of that morning Marc missed four more birds and was about ready to…well, let's just say he "retired' that particular piece of ordnance. He never really told me what he did with it, and I had the uncommon good sense to never ask.

But, oh my. Ghost was absolutely spectacular.

She had done her fair share of sniffing around and pointing birds during the previous couple of years, and had done a pretty damned good job of it. But today was Silver Star Stuff. Not quite Navy Cross. Definitely not The Medal. But very, very good.

Ghost pointed 14 birds—all singles that she had to work hard to find—in less than two hours that morning. She was hot. Runrunrun, WHAM! Locked on point. Marc missed with that dinky little excuse for a shotgun and blamed the leaf cover. She shook her head and took off again.

Bang! Another point. BANG! Another miss. "Sweat got in my eyes," Marc said. Ghost sighed in that way she does and crunched off through the tangle of dead vines and spindly popples and pin oaks.

So it went for the rest of the morning. See, I was trying to let Marc take all of the shots since he wasn't hunting much now that he had a couple of kids.

We were all pretty hot and tired, and some of us were a little bit cranky by the end of the day. But, oh, my. I was absolutely thrilled by Ghost's performance. She was, too, when I finally popped a cap and put some feathers in her mouth.

Marc was figuratively licking the sores on his wounded ego. Ghost was pretty full of herself when we got back to the truck, and even told Ben in no uncertain terms that he was hogging the water dish.

"You, sir, are no gentleman," she told him.

Much to his credit, I thought, Ben stood up a little bit straighter and sounded a lot like Rhett Butler when he looked back with steely eyes and replied, "and you, my dear, certainly are no lady."

No, she most definitely is not.

But she sure had one helluva fine hunt. Very, very fine.

Ghost gave Don Schulz quite an education about the proper way to hunt over a hard-working bird dog, and I got a lot of residual benefits.

Chapter 14

Teaching Was Never Tastier

"Good morning, this is Tony Petrella," I said when I answered the telephone. This was several lifetimes ago, as such things are measured once we start getting a little bit older. Probably sometime back in '92 or '93.

"My name's Charlie Mann," I heard. "Got your name from a guy out at Sage. He said you could help me. I run Hunters Creek Club for my dad, Preston, and we'd like to put on a fly-casting clinic for our members."

That's how it got started. Not the teaching, mind you. I'd been doing that long before I became a manufacturer's rep for Sage rods. What I'm talking about is the chain of events that put me in contact with Don Schulz, and eventually Uncle Magoo—Bill Ross. You'll find out a lot more about him later.

I'd never heard of Hunters Creek Club, which is comfortably nestled in the green rolling hills just a bit east of what has become the dirty gray corpse of Buick City in Flint, Michigan.

Pretty name, Flint. It comes from the days when Chippewa Indians camped along the river and made arrowheads out of flintrock. Pretty country, too, before motorheads clearcut the land so they could build factories to make luxurious Buicks and cheap Chevys.

They finally killed the river by dumping poison into it.

Anyway, this Charlie Mann fellow said he'd pay me to stand next to a couple of ponds on the Club's property and teach some honchos from Dee-troit how to catch stocked trout with flies.

Brother, I couldn't reach for my appointment book fast enough.

Turned out that Hunters Creek Club is a pretty high-falutin' place. Lots of acreage with a big lake, fancy clubhouse, a first-class chef, and a whole bunch of dogs, trainers, and birds. As in pheasant.

Pretty good gig. I even got to take home a few of the dead rainbow trout at the end of the day. Sometimes, a bag of pheasant—picked, plucked, and packaged—went into my cooler along with the fish.

I always got a damned good lunch, too. What's not to like?

This went on for a couple of years and one day a guy who'd been shooting instead of fishing walks up wearing a blaze orange Filson shirt and tells me he's the Detroit advertising manager for *Outdoor Life* and *Field & Stream* magazines.

"I'd like to have a party for the advertising buyers at The Big Three (General Motors, Ford, and Chrysler still *were* the Big Three back then) and the major Detroit agencies. McCann-Erickson, J. Walter Thompson, Young & Rubicam. People like that."

And so for the next several summers I "worked" for Don Schulz at the party Primedia (now InterMedia Outdoors) threw at Hunters Creek Club to schmooze the Motor City magnates.

Finally, one day while I was collecting my paycheck, I mentioned to Don that perhaps he'd like to come up to my house in the woods and shoot some grouse and woodcock. Immediately, his head started nodding like a bobblehead doll with a loose spring.

"Next Saturday works for me," was his instantaneous reply.

His big truck rolled up to my back door at 8:30 in the morning, and we went inside so he could meet Kate. I pulled on my boots, buckled the beeper and bell around Ghost's neck, and we walked around to the front of the house.

"Okay," I said, unhooking the leash. She took off like a streak of white lightning and ran straight down to the tag alders along the river.

She was busy sorting out some scent when we got to the thick stuff. Since she seemed pretty damned serious about it, Don started pushing aside the viburnum bushes and alder saplings.

"Where do you think you're going?" I asked. He looked puzzled. "Down in there with the dog," he replied.

"Nuh uh. That's the dog's job."

"I never hunted over a dog before," he said then. "I guess I was always the dog. What should I do?"

"Well," I said, "right now your job is to wait up here on the edge of the clearing until she goes on point—like that!" The rhythmic beeeeep, beeeeep, beeeeep took us to her. Ghost looked back at me and flipped her head to the side, telling me where the bird was sitting. I moved Don off to the right.

"I'll go in and try to flush the bird in your direction so you can shoot it," I told him. I did, but Don didn't.

"That one got away, sweetie," I told Ghost. "Let's go find another one."

"Easy for *you* to say," she replied, just a little more rudely than I would have liked, considering we had company, but she took off and had another woodcock pinned within two or three minutes. Don missed that one, too.

We followed Ghost south to a huge stand of Norway pines, then cut east from the river to the edge of Frenchman's Swamp. She pointed two grouse, right along the really thick stuff, and Don missed them. I figured a bit of lunch might be a good idea right then.

The water at our house bubbles up from just 50 feet down, but it's as clear and cold as the Manistee River 400 feet away and it tasted mighty good washing down the Monte Cristo sandwiches that Don *still* talks about even after all these years.

That undoubtedly was what gave me the idea for the wild game banquets a bunch of us bushwhackers ultimately started having on the first Saturday in November. I'll tell you about some of them later on. You might even want to try some of the recipes.

Anyway, we sat in the greatroom after lunch and got to know each other a little better while Don examined all of the paintings, drawings, and mementoes Kate and I have accumulated over the years. Since then, Don's brought up some interesting additions. I'll tell you about them later, too.

Well, we finally loaded up gear, guns, and Ghost, and headed south to meet Paul Mesack. You know about him. The vet from Grayling who's always stitching up Ghost's wounds.

After the appropriate introductions of men and dogs, Paul's French Brittany honored Ghost's grouse point a couple of minutes after they stormed the ridgeline opposite our trucks. When the bird flew, its beak nearly clipped Don's left ear.

"Uh, sorry guys," he said. "I didn't see it." Ghost mumbled something impolite, ran down the north side of the hill, crossed the dirt road, and stopped.

"Pointpointpoint" I yelled, and we all three kicked through the weeds, stepped over dead tree limbs and rolled dangerously on the myriad acorns. Shadow was still on the ridge, hoping that another grouse was hiding someplace in all of that old scent.

This time when the woodcock went up I snapped off the Beretta's safety and put the bird on the ground. Ghost needed feathers in her mouth.

A couple of minutes later, working through the tangle of thorny blackberry canes, leafless oaks, and popple branches that clutched at gun barrels and boots, Ghost went rigid and waved her tail at me to move on up. I did. She grinned and jabbed her left front foot toward a thick mess of foliage.

"I'm not shooting," I told the guys. "Fan out on each side and I'll go in behind Ghost." Don missed the grouse that flushed left, but Paul drilled the one on the right, which Shadow (who had finally caught up with us) ran over and grabbed. It was nearly as big as she was, and it was pretty funny watching her half-drag it to Paul.

Later, back at the truck, we gave Don the grouse and wood-cock. When I slapped him on the shoulder and invited him to come back, he nodded once and said, "Next Saturday works for me."

Coming to an understanding of "Who's The Boss" can be temporarily unpleasant for everyone concerned.

CHAPTER 15

OF GROWLS AND GRINS, SORROW AND JOY

I don't know if you've ever held a "Come to Jesus" meeting with your bird dog, but I can tell you right now that it's not a moment in the relationship you later recall with fondness.

Sort of like the time when I was six and thought floral-print wallpaper on the stairway was so boring it would be the perfect place to draw a bunch of pictures. With lipstick. My mother's very bright, very red lipstick.

Or the summer I turned fourteen and decided a couple of the very cute, very "budding" neighborhood girls would like to go for a drive. I got distracted by their "buds" and creased the Buick's right front fender on the garage door frame.

Yes, that would be my mother's very precious, very pale blue Buick. The one with sweeping tail fins, that I completely totaled a couple of years later. But that's another story altogether.

"Come To Jesus." Yes. I can understand why preachers like that phrase. It has an, oh, I don't know, sort of a ring to it that pretty much sums up what's about to happen. Things are going to get ugly. That's certain. So all you can do is close your eyes, gulp hard a couple of times, and wait for punishment.

That's the way it was with Ghost the morning she challenged me.

Flight woodcock from Canada had drifted down the river valleys on the gusty north winds and we'd had pretty good gunning the previous couple of weeks. A lot of points and some exceptionally easy shots had put plenty of feathers into Ghost's mouth. She was feeling awfully smug.

We were barely a mile from the house on that breezy, over-cast day when I let her out of the truck and she was off like a bottle rocket on the Fourth of July.

I heard the "point" mode chirping from her beeper before I even had my shotgun out of its case.

"Kennel-point," I thought as I closed the tailgate. "She can't have found a bird *that* fast." Even so, I slipped a pair of Remington Express 7½ into the Beretta and shouldered my way through the thicket of bare, spindly popple that surrounded a couple of big old cedar trees.

She wasn't taking care of "personal business," though. Nope. She was quivering in intense anticipation because a grouse was ten feet away, hunched down and trying desperately to burrow under a few blades of brown weeds.

The bird was pinned between Ghost on the north and me on the south. I could see that it was young and dumb, and if I did my part he wasn't going to get two minutes older.

After a couple of shuffling steps I stopped and waited. Ghost was a black-spotted porcelain statue. I watched the bird blink. Twice. Finally, it couldn't bear to be center-stage in that scene one second longer and bolted up and away to the west. Briefly.

I took it with the first tube, and it made a soft "thunk" when it bounced once and lay still. "Pretty good way to start the morning," I remember thinking as I reached down for the grouse.

Then I heard a low, deep rumble and froze. "Coyote?" I thought, puzzled. "Naw. Couldn't be."

It wasn't. It was Ghost, telling me with a quivering upper lip to "get away from my bird."

Well. Burton Spiller never prepared me for anything like this. Neither has Frank Woolner. In all of the classic grouse-hunting books that I'd devoured since Colonel Norcross got me into this game, there hadn't been a single word about what to do when your dog decides it wants to be Alpha.

So, I reverted to type and training.

A couple of my uncles, who were cops in Flint, Michigan—which is a very bad place to be a cop, by the way—used to own a honky-tonk north of town. It drew an eclectic mix of cops 'n robbers who tossed back tequila shooters, or shots of BlackJack chased by a draft beer. Boilermakers, the old steelworkers called them where I grew up in northeast Ohio. Except they drank Seven Crown.

Mostly, the nights were peaceful and the only noise came from the really bad, very cheap bands Joe always hired.

Sometimes not.

Occasionally, when they were shorthanded because the regular bouncer was doing thirty days for non-support or something, I'd get "drafted." So, Joe and Doug (who actually are young enough to be my brothers, rather than uncles) showed me a few cop-stuff moves that come in handy during a punch-up.

They also gave me one very important piece of advice. When it becomes inevitable that action is required, always get in the first punch. Invariably, the other guy quickly loses a lot of his enthusiasm.

Which is precisely what happened with Ghost.

Feinting with my left hand, I laid down the Beretta and in one quick, swooping motion I grabbed her collar with my right. Yanking her upright onto her hind legs I stared piercingly into her very surprised eyes and quietly asked if she'd lost her mind.

She blinked rapidly, and gurgled a little bit. I loosened my grip ever-so-slowly and she gulped. Hard.

"Ooops," she said, sheepishly. "Guess I forgot myself for just a second there, Dad."

I stared, with lips compressed and jaws clenched.

"Don't you *ever*," I said slowly, tightening my grip on her collar, "even *think* about doing that again. Do you understand me? You've had a pretty good life with me up till now. If you wanna go live on a farm someplace and sleep in a barn, we can make that happen pretty damn fast.

"It's your choice, Little Girl."

Her eyes went from sheepish to pleading about then. You might not believe this, but I know her eyes filled with tears. This time it was her lower lip that trembled and she sorta sagged all over.

"Dad, I'm sorry. Really, really sorry."

I remembered saying that very thing a long time ago.

I nodded and let all four of her paws feel the moist sand. She sat down, head lowered. I'm not sure if I actually saw a tear fall, or if it was just my imagination.

Taking a long, slow breath, I exhaled and quietly told Ghost, "Let's go find another bird." Her head snapped up and the light came back into her eyes. She smiled and I swept my arm forward as I let out a sharp whistle.

She ran off into the tag alders alongside Frenchman's Creek and almost immediately pointed a woodcock. I shot it and she dug it out of the tall weeds, holding it high for me to see before she dropped it.

When I reached down for the bird, Ghost never moved a muscle. Our "Come to Jesus" meeting was over.

It didn't take Ghost long to realize that it's a lot more fun when we're "pals."

I learned a lot of lessons from John Norcross about hunting and about life.

Chapter 16

Last Hunts and Broken Hearts

Outlined against a pale blue November sky, Ghost and Ben stood alone. Two Centurions surveying Caesar's battleground from the crest of a ridge, awaiting the Legion's charge.

They were tall and proud, and only the white feathering on their magnificent tails whispered in the slightest of breezes. I glanced at Marc, who nodded, then turned to look for his father.

John Norcross was nowhere in sight.

As Marc moved forward, the grouse in front of Ben broke low and right. Almost instantly, the one Ghost had pinned followed like the wingman in a flight of MiG-27s.

When I loosed the proverbial "Hail Mary" shot, a third grouse broke cover and headed for the safety of wherever he called home.

"I guess we'd better find your dad," I said, just as *his* wingman took off and a patternful of Marc's eight-shot grounded that bird for keeps.

Marc was reaching down for his grouse when Ghost's beeper sounded. Another bird took off. I dropped it, and Ghost was very pliant about bringing it to me. For a change.

"I guess we'd better find your dad," I repeated. Marc just shrugged.

"There's a heckuva lot of birds around here. Let's stay on them. He'll find us if he wants to," Marc replied. "We both know how cranky he can be when he's in a snit." True enough.

Marc and I followed the dogs through covert after covert as Ghost and Ben followed their noses. The grouse were acting more like pheasant that morning. In the parlance of a golfer putting on a green, those birds "got legs."

We could hear John tapping out Morse code with the horn on my Tahoe, and I mumbled something about "getting back before he has a fit."

Marc shrugged. "He will anyway, so let's keep hunting. The dogs are looking birdy over by that pine tree."

Ghost and Ben were both on point so I swung to the left behind my Little Girl, and Marc angled right. The bird broke his way and he dropped it.

"BEEEEEEEEEEEP"

"Dammit," I said, "let's get back to the truck before he breaks my horn. These three grouse should mollify him a little bit."

They did. But not by much.

The Colonel grumbled and pouted the whole time I tried to find my way out of wherever we were. I finally got on a paved road that led to home, but I've gotta admit that I never have been able to find that spot again after ten years of trying.

Maybe, in retrospect, that's a good thing.

I was still at the height of my career peddling fishing tackle in those days, and had to make one last swing to Minneapolis. I'd been trying hard to nail down a big deal with the Gander Mountain chain, so the next morning I loaded Ghost into the truck and headed west for one last try at the brass ring.

Gander's fishing tackle buyer at the time (the chain tended to run through them like the Lions went through quarterbacks) was completely ignorant about fly fishing, which had led to some very, uh, unwise decisions on his part.

This turned out to be one of his less-unwise days.

There's an old phrase I'm sure you remember. "Dazzle 'em with your brilliance or baffle 'em with your bullshit." I'm not exactly sure which method worked best for me that time, but I was a pretty happy fella as Ghost and I drove back to Michigan for the last day of grouse season.

After calling Kate to give her the good news I dialed The Colonel's number. He seemed to have gotten over his funk, and said a guy in the barbershop told him about a spot down near CCC Bridge that "always had pats."

"Okay," I told him. "I'll pick you up at first light. Since the forecast is for mid-sixties, we'd better get out early. Boy, the deer opener [always on November 15 in Michigan] is going to be lousy with this heat. Let's hope the last day of grouse season is kind to us."

As usual, Ben whipped around the side of the garage when I pulled into the driveway, and pranced around like a puppy while I dropped the tailgate. One graceful leap and he was nose-to-nose with Ghost, saying "good morning."

As usual, The Colonel was closing the front door even as Ben squirmed into a bunch of towels and settled down for the ride. I stowed John's gear, closed the tailgate, and poured two cups of strong black coffee.

"Where to?" I asked.

"Head to Three C. Wake me up when we get close. I'm tired. My legs hurt. I'm going to sleep. And be quiet, dammit!"

Since there never was any use arguing with The Colonel, I simply did as I was told.

"Hey!" I yelled finally. "We're getting close."

A few more minutes of silence ended when he waved his arm to the left. "Turn here."

I followed the sandy two-track through pine trees that didn't especially look like grouse cover, but kept my mouth shut until we came to a pretty little lake. More like a large pond, really.

"What could they have here," I asked, in my best imitation of the Sundance Kid, "that you would possibly want to shoot?"

John gave me a withering look. "Turn both dogs loose," he commanded. "I wanna watch 'em work together."

Ghost and Ben were off somewhere in the slashings from a fairly recent cutting when I heard her absolutely screaming. "Good God, she must be impaled on a stick! Hold my shotgun," I said, thrusting it at John. "Gotta find her!"

I stumbled and tripped and fell down a couple of times. Ghost ran out of the thick cover, and when I whistled for her to come to me she wasn't bleeding or limping or anything. No trace of why she'd carried on.

"Dammit!" I cursed, "you scared me to death. 'C'mon, let's find The Colonel." Which is when I realized that I'd wrenched my left knee during the race to save her from death.

Ben was sitting at heel when we got back to John.

"I tore up my knee," I told him. "We'd better go home so I can get some ice on it."

John didn't say anything. He just nodded and was quiet the whole way home. We hadn't seen a bird or fired a shot on the final day of grouse season.

I went to deer camp down near Lansing that night despite my twisted knee. Five days later, with a fat doe hung, butchered, and in the freezer—and the truck loaded with Kate and Ghost—I left to spend the next six months guiding fly anglers in Florida.

The days passed quickly in their salty, sun-drenched glory. I caught snook and redfish and tarpon. The Colonel grumped at his hibernation when I called to see how he was getting along.

Now it was June. Kate and Ghost and I had been back in Michigan three weeks. I'd been guiding on the Au Sable or Manistee rivers almost constantly, and hadn't seen The Colonel at all. We'd spoken a few words on the phone, and talked about going fishing when I got an open day.

I had finished yet another guide trip—my eighth in seven days—when I bounced the longboat up the driveway and stopped next to kitchen door.

Kate met me with a concerned look on her face. I had left very early that morning, while she was still asleep.

"Was The Colonel with you?" she asked.

"No, I floated Joe Burke and his son today. They did pretty good. One brown went 18, and two brookies were over 10. Why?"

"Jackie [Norcross] called. So did Steve Sendek. Nobody's seen John all day and they thought you might have picked him up early." I just shook my head and started cleaning the boat with a vague feeling of unease.

The phone rang about seven o'clock that evening. It was my old friend, Pete Stephan. Grayling's Chief of Police. Apparently, John had made a pot of coffee that morning, drank half a cup, left the rest for Jackie, then went out back to feed and water Ben. That's where a deputy found John's body, near the dog that had given him so much joy.

Marc finally arrived from Lansing around midnight, so Kate and I left him with Jackie after a shocking, I guess you could say seismic, eighteen hours.

Kate and I were very quiet on the drive home. Each lost in our own thoughtful turbulence of life, death, and immortality. I bumped past a couple of grouse coverts John and I had loved, and realized it was seven months to the day since our last hunt truly became our Last Hunt.

Suddenly, and with profound sadness, I remembered something Nash Buckingham wrote a very long time ago.

"How kind it is that most of us will never know when we have fired our last shot."

Finally, I cried.

Chapter 17

If Ya' Don't Know, Ya' Don't Know!

I got a phone call from my cousin, Kevin, yesterday. He was gloating about "finally getting out of purgatory." Of course moving back to Flint, Michigan, from Bumsburg, Oklahoma, sounded like a tossup to me.

I let him prattle on a bit, anyway.

"The economy is awfully tough here," he conceded, "but fortunately that did let us get a great deal on a house. We close in a couple of weeks. Till then, Deborah and the kids and I are staying with Mom and Dad." Talk about purgatory!

"And I'm tenth on the seniority list at O'Hare, which is a pretty comfortable spot. Even with the merger, I don't think I'll be affected very much, if at all."

Ah, yes. The merger. United Airlines and Continental, for whom Kevin has spent thirteen years as First Officer and more recently Pilot in Command, had decided to create the country's largest airline.

"I deadhead to O'Hare from Flint or Detroit," he went on, "and fly short hops. An hour or ninety minutes each. Maybe four or five legs a day. Not glamorous, but it pays the bills."

"Thirteen years? How's that possible?" I wondered, *"This whippersnapper got into aviation after listening to my stories about being a pilot and now he's driving birds with wheels behind the cockpit!"*

It made me think back to a morning in northern Michigan nearly ten years ago when I introduced Kevin to an altogether different sort of bird.

He and his new wife had come up to Deward for a weekend not long after they'd gotten married. Kate and I didn't know her very well at the time, so we were happy to have them.

And since I had taught Kevin how to fly fish, call a gobbler, and build a deer blind (plus how to find it again in predawn blackness), this seemed like a good time to introduce him to grouse hunting.

It was still drizzling after a night of hard rain, so I scrambled a dozen eggs, fried a couple pounds of ham, and toasted a loaf of bread. Kevin's a big boy, and grouse don't like to get their feet wet, anyway. So, I wasn't in any hurry.

The women were still snoring indelicately when we finished breakfast, but Ghost was wide awake and grumping by the kitchen door. Every now and then she'd whine, and kick at my boots.

Finally, she loudly yelled that it was time we went hunting. I was afraid Her Royal Redness—meaning Kate—might irritably separate herself from her down comforter and throttle us all, so I agreed. We'd go hunting.

Ghost sat down and tapped her paws on the hardwood floor while I tugged one of my boots out of her jaw. The shotguns and hulls and several gallons of water were already in the truck. The three of us got settled into our respective spots, and I sneaked quietly down the driveway.

"Did you remember to get a hunting license?" I asked. Kevin gave me an "Of course I did!" look. I simply grunted. Once I had guided a guy for three days before finding out he hadn't bought one. Now, I always make sure we're legal before a trigger gets pulled.

"The secret to grouse hunting," I told Kevin, as he tried to empty the thermos into a couple of tall metal mugs, "is quick reaction and leading the bird." He spilled most of the coffee on the floormat, but I didn't say anything. I figured he was nervous.

"Most beginners are so shook up when a grouse thunders out of the brush they stare at the bird and let it fly way out of range before pulling the trigger.

"John Norcross used to give me holy hell for waiting too long. Sure, I've busted up a few birds by getting on them maybe a bit too fast, but you've gotta put lead in the air if you expect a bird to drop.

"Just remember that if the bird goes off low, don't take the chance of hitting Ghost. And, for God's sake, don't shoot me or I'll be pretty damned upset with you."

It was November 10. Woodcock season had been closed nearly a week, and I didn't expect to find any this late in the season at the covert I'd selected. Even so, I put a hand on Kevin's arm and reminded him "grouse only!"

Ghost was fretting in her crate. "Daaaad, let's get moving!"

When I turned her loose, she bolted down into the ravine, dashed up the left ridge, crossed back over to the right ridge, and finally settled on point in the midst of several hawthorn bushes. Perfect grouse cover.

"Here's the plan," I told Kevin. "You move over to the right, into that little opening, so you'll have a clear shot. I'll go in behind Ghost and put up the bird. Remember what I said about reacting quickly."

He did. Too quickly. Fortunately, his shot string trailed far behind the woodcock that twittered off. I was grateful that there weren't any feathers wafting in the light breeze.

"Um, good thing you missed. Remember, woodcock is out of season" I said as gently as I could.

"How was I supposed to know it was a woodcock?" Kevin replied flatly. "I've never seen one before. Or a grouse, either."

"Ah," I said. Just "Ah."

Ghost drank some cold water, slurping and pawing at the collapsible dish, then got back to business. She nosed around the hawthorn bushes a while longer, then started up the far slope.

Kevin and I were 20 yards behind when Ghost stopped. Her magnificently plumed tail curled over her back and her shoulders hunched forward. "Make sure the safety catch is on," I told Kevin, "and move up fast. I'll tell you when to stop."

He did and I did and then the bird couldn't wait it out any more. Kevin raised the barrel as the bird whizzed over Ghost's head and flew straight at us.

"Nonononono!" I yelled. Kevin pulled the trigger. The woodcock kept flying, I tried to shake the bells out of my right ear, and Kevin looked sheepish.

"Don't," I said slowly, "ever do that again."

"Another woodcock?" he asked.

"Yep. And right now I'm going to get a little bit naggy with you. Two things are real important about what just happened here. First, the muzzle blast nearly deafened me. That's bad. Second, if you HAD hit the bird it would have been pulverized."

"So, what should I have done differently?" Kevin asked.

"Well, don't shoot at a woodcock when they're out of season. That's number one. Don't shoot if the barrel is that close to your hunting partner. That's number two. And if the bird had been legal, you should swing around and take it going away so it doesn't explode in a mess. That's number three."

Kevin was quiet while he thought things over. "Do I get another chance, or do we go back home now?"

I draped an arm around his shoulders. "A friend of mine always says 'if ya don't know, ya' don't know.' Well, now you know. So let's see what Ghost is up to."

The ringing in my right ear—which had felt like the Bells of St. Mary's a few minutes before—was mostly gone. I motioned for Kevin to stop walking, and finally picked up the sound of Ghost's beeper off to the right.

"Over there," I motioned. "She's on point. Remember now, if I yell…"

He raised a hand, open-palmed. "I promise," he said. But it was anticlimactic. The bird—of course it was a grouse this time—flew away as we were walking into position and we never had a shot.

Oh, yeah. The real reason Kevin called yesterday was to wish me happy birthday. "I didn't think I'd catch you at home," he said. "I thought you'd be at the cafeteria with all the other old fogies."

"Riiiiiight," I drawled. "And a happy birthday to you, too, punk!" See, we share the same birth date. Twenty-seven years apart.

I haven't seen much of him this millennium, but I suppose that'll change now that he's back in Michigan. I'll probably even take him bird hunting again. After he learns to tell the difference between grouse and woodcock.

It's time he really earned his wings.

Ghost had a fabulous morning pointing woodcock for me and Bill McKellar despite the heat.

CHAPTER 18

SMILE, THO' YOUR BODY'S BROKEN...

When I was a kid growing up in the 60s, my driving force in life was to play football for the Red Dragons. Nothing else mattered. Baseball? Sissy stuff! Schoolwork? An unfortunate necessity to stay on the team! Girls? Well, let's just not go there.

Football was King in my gritty little steel town 60 miles south of Cleveland. It transcended everything else. Every day of every month we ran plays, lifted weights, or watched grainy game films. Nonstop.

If you think the TV show *Friday Night Lights* is hot stuff, you have absolutely no idea what it was like back then. Think cotton in Georgia. Oranges in Florida. Football in Niles.

Undefeated in 63 straight games. Forty-eight straight at home. The stadium seated 15,000 and the place was mobbed on Saturday nights. People were shoulder-to-shoulder wherever they could find a place to stand.

State championships fell on us like snowflakes in a blizzard. To be a part of the team was fabulous enough. To be a starter was sublime.

When the medial collateral and anterior crusciate ligaments in my left knee blew out at the beginning of my senior season, ten years of dreams evaporated with a grinding "crunch."

Dr. Tom Burns scraped shredded cartilage and assorted other crud out of the MCL. But, in those days, they simply didn't know what to do about a torn ACL.

Football doctors called it The Career Killer.

Now it was October 14, 2005. Thirty-nine years after my heart broke on a hot August practice field, my left knee still looked like an overcooked sweet potato. So far, it had let me tenuously wade trout streams and bushwack through thickets, bogs, and deadfalls behind my beloved dogs.

How much longer it would be able to take the pounding was hard to tell. I'd been beating up my body pretty steadily the past few years between guiding and the need for my own time in the woods with Ghost.

I was buying aspirin in Super Size bottles.

A couple of weeks before, on a rainy day that was too miserable to let us hunt, I'd loaded Ghost in the truck and went scouting. Sure enough, I stumbled across some birdy-looking territory.

It wasn't far from a place that had been very, very good for grouse as well as woodcock. It looked exceptionally promising, in fact, and we *always* need fresh coverts.

I hadn't hunted it yet, though, and since I had a day off from guiding, I called Bill Ross and on this beautiful morning we went there with high hopes of what the dogs might find.

Ghost and Ben ran around for a little bit, full of enthusiasm. It wasn't long, though, before they came back and sat down. "There aren't any birds around *this* place," Ghost said. "Let's get outta here."

Ben trooped off after Bill. I told Ghost to go to the truck, and started thinking about another spot near Sand Lake that might hold grouse. "Maybe we'll hit that," I said to myself, lost in thought as I walked, and mostly oblivious to what was happening around me. About the time I was stowing my shotgun, Ghost hopped gamely to the truck on three legs. The other was curled up like a broken banjo string.

"Oh, no. Oh GOD NO!"

Of course, I desperately hoped it was just a sprain. "She probably twisted it. I think I saw her juke around a big blowdown chokecherry tree," I told Magoo. "Let's get her home to rest. I'm sure she'll be fine."

She wasn't.

Ghost slipped, and fell painfully, on the hardwood floor several times. She struggled up as best she could, raised her jaw in that defiant way she has and never whimpered. Not her. Not *ever*.

But it didn't take Enrico Fermi to figure out that she couldn't safely make it up and down the steps to our bedroom in the loft. No nuclear fission problem to solve here.

Paul Mesack wasn't at the Grayling Hospital for Animals when I got there. One of the other docs, Troy Fairbanks, shook her left knee a little bit and gently twisted the joint.

"It's gone," he said flatly. So much for bedside manner.

We hadn't even found a bird that morning, and she was done for the year. Maybe forever.

The very thought that her magnificent career might be over while still in her prime was absolute and total agony for me. I knew what it meant. I'd been there.

I decided a second opinion was in order. In this case, Paul's.

The next morning, to my horror, he verified Fairbanks' assessment. "It's the ACL," Paul said. "You have two options. The first one is something I can do here. It's sorta like stringing a section of hundred-pound monofilament inside the joint.

"It works okay for couch-potato dogs, but you'd be putting her through it for nothing. I've hunted over Ghost. She's so intense she'd probably stretch out that mono in one season. Then we—she—would be right back where we are now.

"The second procedure," Paul went on, "is called a TPLO. You'll have to take her to Michigan Veterinary Specialists. They're down in Southfield. I can set it up for you."

Thirty-six hours later Ghost and I were waiting to see Dr. Joel Alsup.

"What we do," he told me, after wiggling Ghost's leg to satisfy himself the ACL truly was ruptured, "is shave the bones that form the knee joint and essentially restructure it with a stainless-steel plate that's held in place with six screws.

"It'll make the knee at least as good as it ever was if you follow our instructions. But there's no second chance with this.

"You'll have to leash-walk her for eight weeks. If she's loose and chases a critter it's all over. You both lose. Understand? No climbing steps except maybe two or three after about a week. Just to let her go outside. Then gradually increase her exercise time during the next eight weeks. Still on the leash.

"No jumping. No running. Remember. There's no second chance. Okay?"

"When can she go home?" I asked.

"Tomorrow about this time."

I must have looked shocked, because Alsup added, "she'll be groggy, but you can take her home. Just remember…"

I interrupted. "Yeah, no second chance."

The next four months were hard on all of us. Ghost spent most of her time crated so she wouldn't run around or slip or jump onto the sofa or my bed.

Grimacing at the leash, she'd huff loudly—like when I miss an easy grouse shot—and told us in no uncertain terms she wasn't one damned bit happy about all of this silliness. "I'm *fine*, Dad!"

Kate got short-tempered, and so did I. "Frustrated" doesn't even begin to describe the way the three of us were feeling. Sort of like being in a foxhole together, waiting for mortar rounds to land.

KABOOM! Who caught the shrapnel this time?

The only thing that saved us was the simple fact there isn't any snow in Florida, where we spent most of her recovery time. I finally was able to walk her around the neighborhood on a modestly long leash and she could point mourning doves in yards and on the power lines.

Small consolation for both of us, but it was the best we could do under the circumstances. She'd point, I'd throw sticks or pebbles until the birds flew and then yell out "BOOM! We got 'em, Ghost! We got 'em! Let's go find another one." The neighbors thought I was nuts.

Finally, somehow, we were back in Michigan and it was September 15 again.

The temperature was in the high 40s when I met Don Schulz, Bill Ross, and Detroit *Free Press* outdoors writer Eric Sharp, west of Grayling.

It was The Opener and after all those agonizing months Ghost was ready, willing, and—most important—I hoped she was able to hunt. *Please*, God.

She pointed three grouse and eight out-of-season woodcock in less than an hour. Ben, bless his aged heart, found five grouse and three woodcock.

"The dogs found birds quickly," Eric wrote in the Freep a few days later, *"but they almost all flushed out of waist-high ferns*

and bracken, and pines and popples so densely covered in leaves the hunters were lucky to get any more than a glimpse of some tail feathers.

That we never ruffled a single ruff didn't matter one damned bit. At the end of the hunt I sat on the ground next to the truck and nearly wept. My heart was beating hard with a mix of relief and gratitude as I hugged my Little Girl.

Ghost was back!

CHAPTER 19

MAGOO DEFINITELY IS ONE OF A KIND

I'd been wandering around the surgical waiting room about three years when I heard the slurred but unmistakable sound of Bill Ross' voice. I couldn't decipher the words, but I didn't figure he was being very articulate at that moment anyway.

We'd been at Munson Medical Center in Traverse City since six in the morning. His heart catheterization was supposed to have happened at ten. Well, it was ten. At night.

I was trying to decide if my creaky knees could derrick me out of the chair, so I could find out what Bill's situation was, when a nurse walked in. She was smiling.

"Are you the Captain?" she asked, cocking her head to the right.

"I am."

"Well, Magoo—that's what he told me to call him—is back in his room. He's fine, except for being dopey." I literally bit my tongue and said "Thwanks," as she started walking back to wherever.

"He's a real piece of work," she said, stopping and turning around slightly to look at me. "Isn't he." It was a statement, not a question.

"Yep." I guessed she'd already figured him out and didn't need elaboration.

"How long before we ditch this popstand?"

"Give him about an hour. Maybe a little longer. He's talking nonstop, but doesn't make much sense yet. When we decide he's coherent you can take him home."

"How will you be able to tell the difference?" I asked her. She just grinned.

"Ross The Boss," as his subordinates at *Newsweek* Magazine's Detroit advertising office used to call him, came into my life with a whoosh on October 30, 2002.

I had invited Don Schulz to come up from Birmingham to hunt grouse again and, as always, he accepted in a hummingbird's heartbeat.

"You can stay here at the house," I told him. "I'll throw breakfast together, then we can get an early start."

He hedged.

"Uh, my old boss lives in Grayling. We haven't seen each other in a while, and I thought maybe I could reconnect with him. Stay at his place Tuesday night and then meet wherever you want in the morning."

"Sure. I can understand that," I said. Then, in almost an afterthought I added "If the guy's a bird hunter, bring him along."

After a flurry of phone calls, it turned out that Bill lives three blocks from Jackie Norcross. Don and Bill would pick up Ben, then meet me in Deward.

It turned out to be one of those days every upland gunner hates. Ghost and Ben found just one grouse each. The dogs were irritated, and I was frustrated. Don was philosophical. His expectations are never too high when he's hunting birds.

Bill had the time of his life.

"It's been so long since I've been bird hunting! This is wonderful," he said. Several times. "The dogs are great," he said. Several times. "What an absolutely fabulous day," he said. Several times.

What bird hunter can resist enthusiasm like that? Especially the part about "great dogs."

"This was absolutely marvelous and I can't thank you enough," Bill said at the end of the day, as we propped up our feet in the greatroom at my house.

"Glad you had fun despite the lack of participation by the birds," I told Bill. "It certainly wasn't a hunt I'd brag about, but some days are like this. Nothing you can do."

The dogs were curled up on the rugs, snoring and twitching their paws at grouse gone by. Don went out to his truck and came back with a cigar humidor that looks like a shell casing from a Howitzer, and a really classy clock with a painted duck in bas relief on old barnwood.

"Don, these will look great above the fireplace," I said, "but unnecessary."

"Are you kidding?" he said. "It's TOTALLY necessary! You don't know what these hunts mean to me. And now The Boss. To be out in the woods with great friends, hunting over great dogs? This is terrific."

It was nearly a year before Bill Ross hunted with me again.

The flight woodcock were down from the Upper Peninsula on their migration south, and since he'd had such a great time the season before, I called to ask Bill if he'd like to join me and Ghost for a walk in the woods.

He accepted readily.

I killed a woodcock over Ghost that morning, but instead of picking it up and more or less spitting it at me, she whipped around and locked up on another that was 20 feet in front of Bill.

"Shoot it," I yelled, "while I go find mine." Incredibly enough, as I was to learn during the ensuing years, he did. Shoot it, I mean.

Four days later, when Schulz drove back up from Detroit, Ghost was "down" again. This time with a sprained hip. I had been absolutely terrified it was the left knee again. But, Dr. Paul had taken X-rays and insisted that it wasn't serious.

"She'd better take it easy for the next few days," Paul told me. "It shouldn't turn into a real problem, but there's no sense in taking chances."

Bill and Don picked up Ben, and we had a fine time playing with woodcock. I got two, Don got two, and Bill shot his camera. Ghost fumed, and was downright rude to us when we brought those birds into the kitchen to clean.

She twitched her nose at the scent, glared at me reproachfully, limped off to the bathroom and sulked under an old wooden schoolhouse bench. When I took her a dog biscuit she spit it out contemptuously.

Ghost can really be a bitch when she's left behind on a hunt.

I guess that was really the beginning of my friendship with Bill. I'd call, he'd stop at Jackie's to get Ben, then we'd head somewhere in six counties to let the dogs find birds. Sometimes, we even shot one or two.

As the next few years went by, Bill started getting a reputation for missing birds. No, that's not really accurate. He didn't merely miss. He simply never took a shot.

"I never saw it!" he'd wail. "Can you please explain to me how I'm supposed to shoot something I didn't see? You can't. Can you? Where was that bird? Are you sure there really was a grouse that flew out of that tangle? I never saw a grouse fly!"

All I could do was shake my head and apologize to Ghost. And all things considered, I thought she reacted quite civilly. She certainly wouldn't have been that polite with *me*.

"Bill, you really are a product of the advertising business," I told him. "That was pure adverbabble if I ever heard it."

Finally, one morning he showed up wearing a brand new blaze orange cap with MAGOO printed across the front. I have to admit, he did a damn fine imitation of Jim Backus stuttering like the cartoon Mr. Magoo.

Only his eyeglasses aren't as thick.

So, here we were—already into the bird season—when Bill told me about this heart thing. His son, Stephen, lives in Detroit and he has a wife and a couple of kids to deal with, so I volunteered to drive Bill to and from Traverse City on The Day.

Naturally, he protested.

"You've got clients to guide, and Kate and Ghost and that little puppy Heart to tend to, I'll figure something out."

"Listen" I replied, "youd ropped everything to help me find Heart all those times when the little bugger would take off on his own for three hours. Shut up. It's a done deal. I'm taking you."

Seventeen hours after we'd walked through the hospital doors, the docs finally decided it was safe to kick him out of Munson. By the time I pulled into Bill's driveway it was well after midnight. It had been a very long, hard day but he was talkative and mostly rational.

"Get a good night's sleep," I told him, and yawned loudly. "I'll call you in the morning." He started to jabber a little bit more so I said "Goodnight, Bill," and powered up the window while he was in mid-sentence.

I finished the bird season without Bill, who was under pretty strict orders to take it easy, then headed to Florida. He ultimately needed a triple bypass while I was getting fly-flingers into snook and redfish, so the best I could do was call him every couple of days when Ghost or Heart would ask "How's Uncle Magoo?"

"I'm in therapy," he'd say. Thirty or forty minutes later, after a litany that included a bit of sorrowful whining, indignant condemnation of the entire medical field, and hints of resorting to voodoo and/or sorcery, Bill would clam up. "I'll be fine. Pet Sweetie Pie and Shorty Pants for me."

This ritual went on for weeks that stretched into months. Spring passed. Summer came in warm and cozy, turned into a harbinger of fall, and finally settled into the proverbial hot, humid "dog days" that are barely tolerable.

"I just don't have any energy," Bill said when he called one day in late June while I was cleaning the boat after a tarpon trip. "I think maybe I should go to see somebody else about this."

"Good idea!" I replied, maybe just a bit sharper than I should have. I'd already told him in no uncertain terms that whatever medications he'd been taking obviously weren't working and that he'd better get a second opinion. Even a third if necessary.

"Get fixed. One way or another," I said, rather forcefully. "It's three months until Grouse Opener. Ghost and Heart aren't going to put up with any nonsense about you not being able to walk through the woods!"

Whomever he saw or whatever he did during the ensuing month—he's always been a little vague about that—obviously worked. Because one day he finally called me to crow about how good he was feeling.

"The doc gave me a clean bill of health! He said I can play golf, dance the foxtrot [foxtrot?], even run the vacuum cleaner — which I love more than anything, as you know."

"And..." I prodded.

"Oh, yeah. He said I could go grouse hunting when the season opens. If anybody invites me."

A day of hunting sometimes can get so frustrating that the only thing you can do is share a few laughs.

CHAPTER 20

"COMICAL" ALL DEPENDS ON YOUR POINT OF VIEW

My dad got killed in a car accident a few months before my sixth birthday. Mom ran a drill press 40+ hours a week at a small fabricating plant, and you can believe it when I tell you there wasn't a spare nickel for "babysitting," as it was called way back then.

Things were rough, but we managed the logistics okay during nine months of the year. Our Lady of Mt. Carmel School, where I learned this business of writing and reading, was right next to that decrepit old building where tin turned into pop cans, bottle caps, or maybe cheap whistles.

I never did know for sure what the hell they made.

But I only had to walk maybe 50 steps through sunshine, rain, or snow to wait for Mom to finish her seven-to-three shift. And since nearly all the workers were women, I got a lot of pats on the head, candy bars, and an occasional quarter to "go buy some baseball cards."

The question of what to do with me once I was paroled from the Sisters of The Immaculate Heart of Mary for the summer resolved itself pretty quickly.

"You're going to the farm," my mother said that first year, brooking no questions, whining, or alternative suggestions. "Your grandma Bessie's still hurting pretty bad about Dad dying. She wants you there.

"Besides, the hard work will help build your muscles." It was settled. For nearly three months I weeded corn, fed chickens, and milked cows.

I was still too young to plow a field behind the family's one horse, but I learned how to farm.

When the next summer rolled around, Mom announced that I was going to stay in Youngstown with her mother, my grandma Lucy. "You can learn all about Italy." The subject was closed.

So, for nearly three months I rolled cavatelli (properly pronounced ca-va-tell), crimped ravioli, and soaked greens for Italian wedding soup.

I learned how to cook from my dwarfish, roly-poly grandmother. I learned to swear from Grandpa Rock.

It must have been sometime in late June when my mother drove the 20 miles from our house in Niles to eat Sunday dinner at grandma's, and to spend some "quality time" with me.

I don't remember exactly what precipitated my pronouncement—in perfect Italian—of what she could do with the mashed potatoes she was handing to me. Maybe they were dry. Or lumpy.

However, I do clearly remember the moment of shocked silence that sorta stopped everybody in mid-chew.

Then Grandpa Rock laughed like hell. Grandma whooped. Mom turned as red as marinara sauce, grabbed my shirt collar, and dragged me toward the cellar steps and a Fels-Naptha mouthwash.

"Where did you learn that?" she shrieked.

"From Grandpa Rock!"

Now he was laughing so hard tears were streaming down his rough, bristly cheeks. Grandma Lucy was still whooping. Mom was apoplectic and still heading for the basement laundry tub.

"Oh, Mae," Grandma finally sputtered, "leave him alone. He's comical."

I thought about that word—comical—one morning in Deward a few years ago when Ted Kraimer had missed his seventh or eighth woodcock. He'd also swung far, far behind three grouse, including a very makeable double.

Now he dejectedly watched another grouse glide over an old clearcut and disappear into a thick stand of pine trees without having fired a shot at it.

Ghost stared at Ted. I shook my head ever so slightly, warning her to be polite. She sat down then, and slid her eyes sideways to look at me. She does that when she's, shall we say, perturbed.

Ted whispered something that I probably shouldn't repeat here. It was a long string of expletives that he must have learned from an old Navy Chief Bosun'. Or Grandpa Rock. But I thought it was comical.

"These things happen to all of us," I finally said, as soothingly as possible. "I remember when I closed pheasant season one year by missing five straight roosters. Don't worry about it."

Ted glanced at Ghost and winced.

"I can imagine what she's thinking right now. Something like 'here I am busting my tail and he can't hit a bird if it was tied to his nose.'"

Even Ghost smiled at that crack.

I shrugged, gave her some water, and suggested to Ted that we work a little thicket off to the east that most always holds woodcock.

"Are you sure?" Ted said. "Maybe we should just go home and keep my record intact."

I was puzzled. "Uh, what record would that be?"

"This is my sixth time hunting over a dog and I've never shot a grouse or woodcock," he replied, a bit sorrowfully. "I've mostly done walk-up hunting. Usually by myself."

That took me by surprise. It also told me a lot about why Ted was having so much trouble.

"Let's sit on that log," I suggested. "Ghost could use a break, no matter what *she* thinks, and we can talk about this dog business. There are some aspects to it that are completely different from busting through the woods by yourself.

"First, walking behind a pointing dog is absolutely the most enjoyable way to hunt birds. Obviously, you've seen today that she's going to tell you pretty much where the bird's holding. Sometimes a grouse will sneak off like a pheasant, but woodcock hold tight.

"Your job is to determine where the dog's nose and eyes are focused on the cone of scent."

Ted looked at me blankly. "The *what?*"

"It's like an ice cream cone radiating out from the dog's nose," I replied, drawing a rough diagram in the sand. "The most intense scent is at the point of the cone, right under the dog's nose. The farther away the bird is from the dog, the wider the cone gets.

"When the dog locks up tight, you know the bird is hunkered down somewhere close. So, then you move up quickly but carefully, always keeping your feet planted under you and the shotgun ready to be pulled up for a shot.

"The real trick—it took me way too long to figure this one out—is to look for an opening in the trees that lets you position yourself for a decent chance at the bird when it flushes. Assuming, of course, that you've guessed right about its position.

"Then look up in the air—where the bird is going—not down at the ground, because even a fraction of a second counts. And forget all those classic 'swings' you've read about. With Michigan grouse, you poke the barrel toward where you think the bird's heading and pull the trigger. Twice, if you have any doubts at all.

"Don't ever forget that you've got two hulls in that shotgun. Use 'em both. Shells don't cost all that much, and you can't eat 'em at the end of the day.

"There's another important thing that involves flight characteristics," I went on. "I'm an aircraft pilot, and the first thing I learned in groundschool is that you always take off into the wind. That's what gives a plane's wings 'lift' and allows it to fly. A pilot who wants to survive never takes off with the wind at his back.

"Neither do grouse."

Ted nodded. "So, on top of everything else, I have to think about wind direction when I move up on the bird?"

"Yep. But always expect the unexpected. Just the other day Ghost was locked up solid. I tried to read her and the wind as I eased in. I took two steps past her and the woodcock blew out from right underneath her chin. *Behind* me.

"It flew so close to her jaws that she almost caught it in midair. Then it stayed low and I couldn't take a shot without killing her. That was one smart bird. Or just damn lucky. Either way, it's still flying."

"Yeah," Ted said, "just like all of these birds today. I can't *believe* Ghost has pointed so many and I haven't managed to knock one down."

"Let's go work that little thicket now," I suggested, "and see if some of the things I just mentioned are any help."

Ghost took off in a white blur when I whistled and waved my arm. She knew exactly where to go. Within two minutes a supercharged blast of woodcock scent hit her in the face. She slammed into a point so fast that she looked like a cartoon character.

"Get up next to her on the right side," I urged Ted. "Look for an opening in the trees and be ready to shoot." I hung back and watched.

A limit of woodcock whistled up and tried to get away. Ted picked the one in the middle and fired once. It was obvious he wasn't going to need the second tube.

Then Ghost did something strange.

I was walking over to congratulate Ted when she picked up the bird. Usually, she'll hold it up for me to see, spit it out, and get back to hunting. Occasionally, she'll bring it to me as an excuse to ask for some water so she can rinse the loose feathers out of her mouth.

This time, she walked back to Ted, dropped the woodcock at his feet, and smiled. Ted smiled back at her. I smiled at them both.

"I'll be damned," Ted said softly. "I'll be damned." His streak had ended. He was a full-fledged bird hunter at last.

CHAPTER 21

LIFE AND DEATH ARE ONLY A WHISPER APART

Pete Sykes is one of those guys any fly angler would like to be. He can cast a mile of 12-weight line, and still fits into a pair of size 26 shorts. He's the proverbial "been there, done that, came home with the commemorative coffee mug" fella who always lands the biggest fish on the teeniest leader on a fly that he invariably tied the night before.

Without eyeglasses.

So we're down in North Captiva Pass one morning. It's dawn and already over 80 and by-cracky if this ain't gonna be one nasty hot mother of a day to be out here at the south end of Charlotte Harbor looking for tarpon.

It's flat calm and the water's a blue-green color so clear that it's like you can see forever. And quiet. Like being at High Mass when His Eminence The Bishop Cantarucci pauses justthatlong before telling us in Latin to "go and sin no more."

I'm up on the platform. The pole's useless, of course, in 20 feet of water. But I'm figuring maybe I can see something coming down the chute that funnels eastward through The Pass.

I do.

"Pete, we've got a bunch heading right at us. They're happy fish. Slopping around like they just got let out for recess. I'm down on the deck. It's all up to you."

The appropriate thing right now would be to say that Pete stabbed a big pig on that slinky, sexy-looking black-and-purple streamer he was casting, and armwrestled it boatside 30 minutes after she nearly pulled his arm out of its shoulder socket. That would be nice. In fact, that would be heroic.

It also would be a lie.

A dozen, maybe two dozen tarpon swam past the boat. Hell, it mighta been a hundred. Even all these years later I'm still surprised they didn't gang up and just flip us over for the helluvit.

Instead, they simply ignored us. They ignored Pete's fly, and they most assuredly ignored all of my entreaties to A Higher Being. I don't know what poker game they were heading for, but they certainly never bothered to play with us. Maybe our table stakes weren't high enough.

Frankly, I was more than a little bit pissed off.

"Hey! Toss me some water," Pete called from the bow when they'd left. "These damn fish aren't worth getting killed over. I nearly had that happen once before. Never again, buddy. Gotta stay hydrated."

I don't recollect all of the details, but Pete told me he had been somewhere in Belize or Costa Rica several years before and he was concentrating too much on fishing and not enough on staying alive.

"Young, dumb, and stupid," he said, shrugging.

Bottom line is when they finally got him back to the lodge it was obvious that he was really close to dying from heatstroke. "They put me in the bathtub and started packing me in ice," Pete said. "And you *know* how precious ice is in the tropics. It lowered my body temperature and saved my life."

So a few years later I'm someplace around Baldwin, Michigan, with Don Ingle and his big old Lab named Socrates. Ghost had hunted the first two coverts, and we'd shot at but never seriously molested a couple of woodcock.

She was grumbling, like she always does when I make her quit hunting, but I stuffed a couple of Alpo Liver Snaps into her mouth, gave her a big drink of water, and told her that it was Soc's turn and that she should just shut up and take a snooze.

We hiked back into the woods and Don peeled off to my right. Soc was lumbering along toward my left shoulder maybe just 10 minutes after he'd started pounding through the trees. "WHOOOOK." I heard. *"What the hell,"* I wondered. "AAAAACCCKK!!!" gave me the jitters.

Then I looked at Soc. His tongue was purple, and hanging out the side of his mouth. His eyes were bulging.

"Don! Your dog's having heatstroke. Come quick!"

We poured water into Soc from a bottle in my vest, but it was obvious that we needed a lot more—fast.

"Here's the rest of the water I had in my vest, " I told Don. "I've got several gallons in the truck. Gimme your shotgun. I'll be back as fast as these old knees will let me. You take care of Soc."

I hobbled back with several more flasks and we poured water into and over Socrates. It looked as if it might even have been helping.

"I'll go bring the truck as close to the gate as I can," I told Don. "Walk Soc back as quickly as he can go."

Everything was ready. Truck pulled tight to the walk-in. Door open. More water waiting. Everything except Don. And Soc. I crab-walked back down the lane and saw Soc lying on the ground. Don was standing over him, looking dazed.

"I don't think he's gonna make it," Don whispered.

"Dammit! Take off your hunting vest," I yelled. "He's GOTTA make it!"

And so two aging bird hunters wrestled an even more aged Labrador retriever out of the woods by alternately carrying and dragging a tattered old orange hunting vest that was trying mightily to support 100 pounds of nearly dead weight.

When we got to my truck I told Don to get into the passenger's seat. Then he pulled and I pushed Soc onto the front floor as if he were a big burlap bag full of flour. Off we raced.

My 911 call to a sympathetic operator turned up the fact that the only veterinarian within 30 miles was Don's own—in Evart, Michigan. Soc would never make it.

As we sped past Club 37, a restaurant renowned for its huge and succulent prime rib dinners, a memory flashed into my brain pan and both feet slammed down on the brake pedal.

ICE!

Thirty seconds of explaining to the three women working the bar and restaurant was all it took. I loaded teeny ice cubes into a five-gallon bucket and poured them through the truck window.

Two, three, four, five buckets of ice filled the front floor of the Tahoe and covered Don's legs and Soc's convulsing body. Meanwhile, one of the good ladies brought bar towels soaked in cold water to drape on Soc's head and shoulders.

By the time we reached the vet clinic Soc was able to walk in on his own. The vet, a woman, checked him over, pumped in vitamins or something and we headed back to Don's hunting cabin.

Naturally, we fussed with Soc and got him settled.

"I've got single malt," Don told me. "Help yourself."

"You have a willing and needy customer," I replied. Tossing it back, I carried the glass with me while I headed for the door.

"I'll let Ghost out of her crate for a walk, and then top this up and throw together some chow for everybody," I told Don.

Understandably, he was only half listening. After all, he'd come within a whisper of losing his best friend.

Outside, I hoisted Ghost out of the crate and set her on the ground. "Okay," I told her, "Go for a walk."

She looked at me and blinked. Then she hobbled off a few feet and squatted. As best she could with one leg dragging. "Beautiful," I thought. "Just beautiful. Soc damn near died and now Ghost can't walk. God only knows what *this* is all about."

I carefully lifted her back into the crate and sighed heavily.

Then I fished a few ice cubes off the floor of my truck, flicked away some dog fur, bits of leaves and a couple of ants. Plunking the cubes into the empty glass I stared balefully at Ghost and walked back inside the cabin.

"Gimme that bottle," I told Don. "Looks like we're *all* done hunting." Then I ruined a very healthy measure of very good Scotch whisky by pouring it over the cubes, and sat down with a groan.

It had been that kind of day.

Guiding grouse hunters is a lot of fun most of the time, but there are days that can try the patience of the dog as well as the guide.

Chapter 22

The Days of Our Guides—One Big Soap Opera

I got a telephone call from Ray Schmidt one evening nearly 30 years ago. We exchanged pleasantries, swapped lies about steelhead we'd caught—or lost—and gossiped about the curious mix of fishermen, bandits, and bums who inhabited Wellston, Michigan, back then.

Finally, Ray hit me with a bombshell.

"You asked me once how a guy gets to be a sales rep in the fly fishing business," he said. "I told you to either get hired by an established group, send out cold-call letters trying to convince manufacturers to hire you, or buy an existing territory."

"Do you want to buy mine?"

I was, to borrow an old-time phrase, "flummoxed."

"Why," I asked, "do you want to stop repping?"

"The travel," Ray replied. "I'm tired of being on the road all the time. I just want to stay here and guide fly fishermen on the Manistee and Pere Marquette for trout and steelhead."

My initial reaction was that he'd gone crazy. Guiding every day? Getting up at o-dark-thirty to shove around a boatload of guys who still called the rods "poles" and the fly line "string?"

Well, if he was going nuts, I was at least willing to hear his pitch.

Several sit-downs later, and after some serious discussions with Kate, it was decided that, yes, effective New Year's Day 1986 I would own the Olson Creek Company. Which basically gave me the temporary right to represent Winslow Manufacturing in the Midwest.

In other words, Sage fly rods.

Twenty years later, it was "déjà vu all over again," as Yogi Berra once was quoted as saying.

Only this time I was the one telling John Bueter "between splitting my time between Michigan and Florida, and my guide business growing so much, I just think it's time to get off the road.

"Do you wanna buy my territory?" He did.

Which meant that because I wasn't doing my dog-and-pony show throughout six states during the fall—by now for Temple Fork Outfitters fly rods—I could guide grouse and woodcock hunters in addition to my stable of trout and tarpon anglers.

Ghost was ecstatic.

So was I. Mostly.

It was sunny on this Tuesday morning, my first guide trip of the hunting season. We'd been out scouting, of course, and on opening day we had found so many birds that when Eric Sharp wrote about Ghost's exploits in the Detroit *Free Press* the phone immediately started ringing. I'll tell you about the Bump Brothers shortly.

Anyway, this day I had a guy from Traverse City and his pal from Wyoming. The flight woodcock were down from Canada, and birds were everywhere. Ghost "played like a champion" in every sense of the word. She put up 11 grouse and 18 woodcock, but my shooters only put two and three, respectively, on the ground.

I just couldn't get the guys to pull the trigger.

"Why didn't you shoot at that grouse?" I quietly asked Dick, while we watched it juke through the pine trees like an F-16 eluding heat-seeking missiles. I could hear Ghost grumping and tried to shush her.

Dick looked at me and shrugged. "I was waiting for that 'certain' shot," he finally said.

"Uh, Dick, the only thing that's certain," I told him, "is that if you don't put lead in the air nothing's going to fall." He nodded in understanding, and later managed to collect two woodcock. Pat, meanwhile, dropped two grouse and one woodcock.

The very next day was shaping up to be a repeat performance. There were plenty of birds around, and Ghost was finding them. Oh, was she ever finding them.

I simply couldn't convince my "sports" that they needed to pull the trigger more quickly and more often. Of course, one of them did have a legitimate excuse. He was missing his trigger finger.

"I lost it in an accident when I was a kid," Rod said, "so I have to slide my middle finger past the trigger guard before I can take a shot."

Oh.

His son-in-law, Steve, had fished with me during the summer, and thought a walk through the October woods would be a very fine thing.

They drove over from Traverse City, and we met west of Grayling to start off at a couple of my favorite spots. Ghost was on the ground first. She pointed a grouse and three woodcock, and we had two more wild woodcock flushes, in less than an hour.

Neither man popped a cap until I had Ghost leashed and we were walking the old logging road back to the trucks. Then she pulled one of her classic "Whoa, whoa, Dad!" routines, stubbornly pointing into the brush with her chin.

"Um, I think somebody should load a shotgun and get ready to take care of business," I said. Steve and Rod looked at each other. Then at me. Then at Ghost.

"Seriously," I prompted. "She's not kidding."

So Steve slipped a couple of hulls into his Remington. I took two or three steps off the road. Ghost stopped and leaned forward with her jaw tightened and her eyes blazing.

Up went the bird. Boom went the shotgun. Down went the bird.

"Sonuvabitch," Steve swore softly.

"I'll be damned," Rod concurred.

"Here," I told Rod, handing him the leash. "Hold Ghost or she'll be off looking for more. I'll get that woodcock."

We walked down the road a quarter-mile after we'd all admired Steve's woodcock and told Ghost what a magnificent hunter she is. At the truck, she barked for a couple more Alpo Snaps, pawed furiously at the water dish to cool off, and hopped up into her crate for a snooze.

Now I was putting the bell and beeper on Abner, and Ghost was getting thoroughly agitated. Abe belongs to Rex Farver by way of an old-timer who went into a nursing home that didn't see the value of having English setters hanging around. Unfortunately, Abe doesn't get to hunt much.

But, all I had left of good old Ben was his ashes, and I needed another dog to spell Ghost. Heart was still falling all over his own feet, and wasn't anywhere close to being a bird dog. But, we'll get to all of that later.

Abner was five, and had done some preserve hunting. Alas, he was full of vinegar and absolutely bursting with the sort of energy common to his breed. Especially after being penned up for weeks. He wanted to run!

Abe did manage to point a woodcock and bust two more, but then he ran away and it took forever to find him so I slammed the door on his hunting day when I finally did manage to grab him.

By the time we got to the next covert Ghost was hopping mad. She pointed two grouse and five woodcock, and we had two more woodcock flushes, in the 79 minutes we hunted. Eighteen birds flew. Only two fell.

She gave me hell all the way home.

A couple of days later, Geoff and Greg Bump hunted with us for the first time. "We read that article in the Freep," Geoff said, "and decided we need help. We can find woodcock all day long, but we never put up any grouse!"

Over coffee, we talked a bit about what they'd been doing and where they'd been doing it.

"It sounds to me," I finally said, "that you're hunting in habitat that hasn't held a grouse for two months. Those bare, spindly popple trees aren't feeding grouse now, and they certainly don't provide any cover.

"C'mon. Let's take a walk."

We skirted the edge of a huge blackberry thicket, and I noticed the nervous glances they were tossing at each other. It was clear that they weren't sure if they were in the right place with the right guide.

Then Greg's Brit stuck her nose into the thicket and a grouse busted out of the thick, purple canes. Greg dropped it with his first shot and let out a giddy whoop.

Geoff whipped his head toward me and shouted, "Did you *really* expect to find a grouse in there?" He looked just a little bit wild-eyed.

I shrugged. "That's what we're here for, isn't it?"

Greg had picked up his bird and was admiring it. "We never, ever, would have hunted this cover," he said.

"Not in a million years," Geoff added, shaking his head. "Why are we here? Why are the *grouse* here?"

I smiled, then. Because I remembered asking John Norcross that very thing several years ago. And I tried to be just as patient and uncondescending with Geoff and Greg as The Colonel had been with me.

"Take a good look around," I told them. "Besides all the little clumps of trees and thick weeds, this place is covered with blackberry canes. Grouse love the fruit, eat the leaves, and burrow down to hide from hawks that certainly won't fly through all those thorns.

"You find blackberry patches, you'll find grouse."

Days like that make it fun being a guide. The guys saw six grouse and nine woodcock in cover they admitted "we wouldn't have spent ten minutes hunting—if at all."

Then there are days like the one I had with Bob.

He was the chief financial officer (CFO) for several big companies after leaving Chrysler. He's an exceptionally polite man, and owns some very nice shotguns. Except he never shoots anything with them.

Ghost was pointing grouse and woodcock bing-bing-bing and Bob never fired a shot. Finally, she came over for a drink of water, flopped down on the cool deer moss, and begged me to find out what his problem was. "Feathers!" she wailed. "I need feathers in my mouth."

"Say, Bob!" I called. No response. "Bob?" Still no response. I walked over and tapped his shoulder and he jumped, startled. "Uh, Bob…"

"Wait a second," he said, pulling out the foam ear protectors he was wearing. I started to talk and he waved me off, taking two tiny hearing aids from his shirt pocket.

"Sorry," he said, "my hearing's terrible. I'm trying to protect what's left of it by finally using these earplugs. Shoulda started with them when I was a kid. Wouldn't be in this fix now.

"What'd you wanna tell me?"

"Uh, nothing, Bob. Just wondered if you want some water."

Ghost found nine grouse and nine woodcock that day. Bob shot at just one bird, far too late, and missed it.

He did, however, go home with dinner. Ghost found a cripple on our way back to the truck and was so mad by then that she ran it down, bit its neck, and threw it onto the ground at our feet.

As we were packing the grouse into a cooler, Bob mentioned that he was going in for cataract surgery the next week. "Maybe that will help improve my shooting a little bit."

When I got back home and told Kate about the day's events she set down her ever-present mug of super-octane coffee and stared at me. Sorta shocked.

"So, what you're telling me," she finally said, incredulously, "is that you and Ghost just spent the whole day guiding a guy who's legally blind and deaf.

"And then you *wonder* why he only shot at one bird?"

Despite her tutelage from Ben, Ghost remained intolerant of most other dogs.

CHAPTER 23

STRANGERS IN THE HOUSE, GHOST HAS...

Sarasota is a few miles north of where I usually guide fishermen during the winter to earn a living. Turns out, it was the first city in the United States to create a leash-free park for dogs.

Somehow, somebody convinced the city commissioners to find enough money to buy seven acres of vacant land, chain-link fencing for the whole thing, a hookup to pipe in water, and several thousand plastic "sanitary bags." The Parks Department even brought in a few picnic tables, and covered them with shed roofs to give the humans some shade while the dogs ran.

Back in Niles, where I grew up, the old guys playing cards at Bagnoli Hall, or Bella Napoli, would have winked at each other and nodded. Maybe rubbed a thumb against a forefinger. One *paesan* to another, ya know? But, hey, I ain't here to throw stones when I don't know what I don't know for certain.

After all, Sarasota has more millionaires per capita than anyplace else in America—*including* Palm Beach. Think about THAT while you pour another Scotch!

What I do know is that word of the park's popularity spread throughout the country awfully fast. Today, cities and towns all over America have them. At that time, it was a 20-mile drive each way for me to take Ghost there. But I figured outings like that would be wonderful for my new puppy.

Ghost was less than a year old the first time we drove to the 17th Street Park. The parking lot was jammed with Jags and Beemers, and inside the fence dozens of dogs were chasing each other all over the place. "This is *great*," I remember thinking to myself. "Ghost will be able to run like hell and meet lots of other dogs."

She certainly did. But not in the manner either she or I wanted.

Poor Ghost had a very happy, expectant grin on her face when I opened the gate and ushered her inside. "WOW, Dad," she said, "this is gonna be fun!"

That lasted, oh, about as long as it took for a pack of very large, very bully-type dogs to realize there was "fresh meat in the prison yard."

They charged us like the Lakota Sioux swarmed over Custer's Seventh Cavalry when Crazy Horse and Sitting Bull nodded at each other and agreed "Now!"

We were totally engulfed by barking, yelping, growling dogs. Ghost got knocked down and three or four big ugly mutts were all over her.

"SCAT," I yelled, flailing the leash I was holding. "SCAT!"

One by one, their owners sheepishly sorted out and collared this horde of gangsters while I regained my composure.

Ghost gathered her wits and got to her feet. She wasn't smiling anymore. In fact, she was pissed off. She didn't say anything, though. Just stared after them with a cold glare.

Unfortunately, that episode set the tone for her attitude toward other dogs from then on. She'd vaguely tolerate them if they kept their distance. When they invaded her comfort zone, she curled her lip menacingly. Her message was abundantly clear.

If they ran toward her growling, she preemptively bit their noses quick as a cobra. BANG! End of "discussion." One time a "rescue" greyhound ran her over at the Venice dog park. She came up fast and hard, and when the dustup was over my share of the vet's bill for stitching up that long-legged dummy was 80 bucks.

The only dog Ghost ever took a shine to at the park was Stella, a shy little Gordon setter bitch that belonged to Mary Gospodarek. Her son, John, ultimately became my partner in Florida for guiding fishermen.

Ghost and Stella would play together and wrestle and generally have a wonderful time. But heaven forbid another dog tried to horn in on their play or menaced Stella. Ghost simply wouldn't tolerate it.

I finally had to quit taking her to the park. It just got too complicated. Besides, Mary moved to North Port, ten miles away, and quit bringing Stella.

So, you can imagine the trepidation about bringing another dog into our house. Kate and I agonized over that question for three *years*. Finally, Rex Farver suggested we get a male, since Ghost did seem to flirt with the guys.

"I think you'll be surprised at how well she adapts," Rex said. "Look at how she and Ben always got along. I really don't think it'll be a problem. Plus, you really do need to break in another bird dog."

He was right.

Roni and Bill Worrix had quit breeding setters and moved to someplace in Tennessee, so they were out of the equation. I really wanted another dog from the Ghost Train line, but it just wasn't working out.

Finally, I heard about a fellow in Jonesville, Michigan, just south of Jackson. There was a lot of Crockett blood in his dogs' lines, as well as some Grouse Ridge and Amos Mosley boys and girls. One was the national champion runner-up.

I drove down to look at the dam and sire.

They hunted well on some planted quail, and the timing for getting the puppy would mostly work. I wrote out a $100 deposit check, and waited for word of a successful "coupling."

Finally, I got the call. As it happened, I was down in that area visiting a couple of fly shops, so I drove over to the kennel. The pups were six days old and their eyes weren't open yet. They looked like a bunch of little moles.

I watched them blindly fight for a nipple, and was impressed with one little fellow. "Let me hold him?" I asked. Momma didn't object. "Yeah," I said after a minute. "This one."

"There's another guy who's got pick of the litter and he wants a male, too," John Griffith said, "but he's partial to liver-and-white instead of tricolors like this one. I think you'll be okay."

I looked at the heart-shaped blaze on his forehead and *his* name was sealed right there on the spot. "His name is Heart. Manistee River Heart," I told Kate, calling her even as I started driving home.

"Now let's just start praying Ghost doesn't kill him the first day!"

We took Ghost with us when we went for the puppy. Better, I thought, that they meet on neutral ground. After a lot of tentative sniffing Heart fell asleep on Kate's lap. Ghost laid down in her crate, but looked awfully dubious about what was happening.

Only one of us slept on the three-hour drive home, which was punctuated with roadside stops every time Heart woke up. As a friend who breeds Salukis told us many years before, "when a puppy wakes up, a puppy has to pee." Good advice.

Only one of us was full of "vim and vigor" when we finally rolled into Deward. Ghost sulked and went looking for mourning doves under the feeders next to the garage. The puppy blundered around the house. Kate and I exchanged nervous looks when Ghost came in and grumped over to the food dish.

Sure. It finally happened.

Full of unbridled puppy enthusiasm Heart yipped once and made a dive for her leg. Intent, I suppose, on showing Ghost how much he loved the dog he obviously considered his surrogate mom.

Ouch!

Ghost whipped around in what I took to be stunned surprise. I started to yell, held my breath, and looked at Kate. She pretty much was in the same shape I was in. Panicked.

The puppy shrieked when Ghost hit him. But I noticed she had head-butted him.

Teeth weren't involved, but Heart was shocked. None of his brothers or sisters had ever done this to him. He cried piteously while Ghost went back to her food dish.

Heart finally calmed down, but kept looking nervously at Ghost the rest of the night. Next morning we were all outside. I was fussing with some fly rods, Ghost was stalking birds, Kate was planting flowers, and Heart decided to find out what marigolds taste like.

"Heart!" Kate yelled, "NO! Those belong to Mom!"

Like a streak of white lightning, Ghost materialized from under the canopy of ferns and sent Heart rolling like a furry black, white, and brown bowling ball. And that finalized, for all time, the pecking order.

I already told you a little bit about Abner, and how I borrowed him from Rex Farver for that hunting season when Heart was just a gangly kid. Kate and I were more than a little worried about how Ghost was going to react to *two* new dogs in the house, but it had to be done.

As it turned out, Ghost mostly ignored both of them. At first.

"The Boys," as we started calling them, had a ball together. The house was absolute chaos, of course, but Abner really did a marvelous job of "socializing" Heart.

They wrestled. They bounced off the furniture and off the walls. When they had a contest to see who could pee the highest on a fence post in the dog pen, poor little Heart fell over sideways into the dirt.

Finally, one day Ghost had enough and tried to join in all the puppy games. "The Boys" ignored her. Kate and I watched day after day with raised eyebrows as Ghost tried and tried to get in on the fun.

They still ignored her.

At the end of October it was time for Abner to go home to Indiana. Heart stood on a window seat in the kitchen, watched Abner jump into the back of Rex's Tahoe, and never moved as it went down the driveway and curved out of sight.

Heart stared after Abner for a long time. Kate and I didn't say a thing. Then Heart's head snapped around and looked at each of us. It seemed as if there was understanding in his eyes.

Slinky as a cat, he eased off the window seat and nudged up against Ghost. She stood very still for a couple of heartbeats, then whirled around, grabbed his collar with her teeth, and wrestled him across the kitchen.

Heart wasn't a stranger any more.

Chapter 24

Running Like the Wind...With the Winded

The analogy going through my mind on November 12, 2007, was of Viper and Maverick turnin' and burnin' someplace over the California desert. Out where doing something stupid isn't going to result in what military people refer to as "collateral damage."

Except, instead of Viper (Tom Skerritt) dusting the young hotdog Maverick (Tom Cruise) in the movie *Top Gun*, this was Ghost and Heart in Real Life.

We were down in Kalkaska County. Camp Grayling's automatic weapons range was to the east and the sound of freedom was roaring from .50 caliber machine guns. Off to the west, I could almost hear the sound of rushing water and rising trout in the Manistee River.

Jim Powers and Bill Ross were jawboning the way only a Michigan "Old Blue" and an MSU "Sparty" can do when in such close proximity to each other. Especially since Michigan had beaten MSU 28-24 in football just the week before.

They couldn't hear anything except each other.

Personally, I didn't give a damn about the game either way. Besides, I was too busy sorting out and attaching various bells and beepers to the dogs.

It was the first time Ghost and Heart were going to hunt together, and I was as nervous as a virgin on his wedding night.

I turned the dogs loose with a whispered prayer. I didn't know what to expect, so I feared the worst and hoped for the best. The worst, of course, would be Ghost murdering the puppy if he tried to muscle in on one of her "kills."

Well, murder might be too strong a word, I thought. But surely there would be blood, and then the issue would be whether Heart would ever want to hunt again. With or without Ghost. What a dilemma.

Ah, cut it out, I said to myself. *"The worst thing that really might happen is that Heart takes off and I never see him again. Then I drive to Alaska or Montana, because I couldn't ever go home and tell Kate I lost the puppy."*

Well, none of that happened. What I did experience was nothing short of a miracle. If I wrote a movie like this, the boys in Hollywood would turn me down flat. And laugh like hell while lobbing my script into a trash basket.

Believe it if you will, or call me a liar, but right here in my hunting log it says that when I whistled and waved my arm and turned both of them loose Ghost struck point 20 yards from the truck.

We'd been hunting for about 98 seconds!

Hell, the puppy never had *time* to decide whether or not to run off. Ghost was radiating energy like a nuclear reactor and Heart's immature brain was trying mightily to sort out everything that was going on.

Technically, I guess you could say that Heart instinctively "honored" Ghost's point. At least, that's what I'd *like* to believe. Truthfully, though, I figure he was terrified to come closer than 15 feet. I'm sure the marigold episode was firmly fixed in his mind.

I loosed both tubes at the flush, and stood staring in frustration as two more grouse blasted out of the brush. I had an empty shotgun, and Ross was still berating Powers about how "the Weasels stole that game from MSU."

Neither of them even knew grouse were flying.

Heart's enthusiasm finally got the better of him and he rushed forward, flushing a woodcock that up to now had gone unnoticed by everybody. Unfortunately, it was at that moment Ross snapped out of his tirade and yelled "woodcock!" at the instant he fired.

It was a pretty damn fine shot, I must say. The unfortunate part was that woodcock season had closed exactly a week prior. Ooops! A "Magoo-Do-Do."

We decided to quit on that, uh, note.

The next morning was overcast and the temperature was in the mid-40s. Basically, a perfect day for bird hunting.

Bill and I drove a few miles west of the house to a favorite covert. We'd been careful to hunt it sparingly, so I was pretty sure there'd be some grouse holding in the thick tangles.

I reminded Bill that woodcock season was still closed, and turned loose the dogs.

Heart was ecstatic to be hunting with Ghost again, but couldn't decide if he should try to keep up with her (he couldn't), or stick close to me. I (mostly) got the nod.

Ghost found a pair of grouse not long after she started nosing around, but I missed the first one and Ross wailed "I never saw the second bird." That's my Magoo!

Both dogs watched, a bit dejectedly I thought, as that second grouse flew away. Typically, Ghost clenched her jaw and started looking for more scent.

She ran like the wind. Poor Heart tried vainly to keep up with her, but his gangly legs were flopping all over the place and tripping over branches. His eyes were wide and his tongue was purple when Ghost turned into a statue.

I'm pretty sure Heart was grateful that he could stop chasing after her. He was so winded that he "honored" Ghost's point by sitting down. When I shot the bird he struggled to his feet, but kept his distance.

Ghost paraded around with the grouse in her mouth for a minute, showing off, but I really couldn't blame her for rubbing it in just a little bit. As they say in the military, Rank Hath Its Privileges.

Besides, we only had one more day of bird hunting, then she had a date with Michigan Veterinary Specialists to have the metal plate in her left leg removed. It had become infected two years after her TPLO surgery, and she kept "worrying" it.

Very early the next morning we drove to Mike Beatty's farm in Laingsburg. He'd invited me to come down for the deer opener again, so I figured we could put the dogs out on Mike's quail and let them all run around like crazy to close bird season, then do some deer hunting the next day.

After about an hour of watching them crash through the tall grass, rooting out quail, it was obvious that the puppy was plum played out. Ghost, of course, wanted to keep right on hunting.

But, it was time to load up the dogs and head to the vet's office in Southfield. Heart wasn't sure why we drove back to Mike's without Ghost, and had a worried expression in his beautiful brown eyes. In fact, he stuck awfully close to me the rest of the night.

He was still confused the next morning during his "consti-
tutional," but settled into his crate without much fuss when Mike
and I headed out to the deer blinds in the moonlight.

I shot my deer that afternoon. After getting it field-dressed
and hung, I made myself as presentable as a Jackpine Savage
(that's what they call us Up North Michigan guys) ever gets.

Heart and I drove back to Southfield for Ghost, and the
little guy was absolutely ecstatic when he saw her, whimpering
and slamming himself against his crate. It was the first time they'd
been separated.

When we got back to Mike's I helped her down out of the
crate and snapped on her leash. She strained against it and whined.
"Lemme go get some more birds," she implored. Heart sniffed at
Ghost's stitches apprehensively, took a couple of quick steps backward and looked at me with big, questioning eyes.

Ghost regally ignored him. It was full dark and she still
wasn't completely recovered from the knockout gas but she wanted
to go hunting. "Just like all setters," Mike said, chuckling. "They
never quit."

"Well, Ghost might not like it very much, but Dad says
it's time for a rest. C'mon, kids," I told them. "The next quail you
chase will be in Florida. This bird season is officially closed!"

Heart learned his lessons quickly and came to love the taste of feathers in his mouth as much as Ghost ever did.

CHAPTER 25

GRUDGINGLY PASSING THE TORCH OF GREATNESS

Forty years ago—my God, can it *possibly* be that long ago?—I was a sportswriter at the *Palm Beach Post*. My "beat" was the Miami Dolphins, and at that particular moment nobody considered it a very choice assignment. Except me. I was thrilled.

I didn't give a damn that the 'Fins had won just four games the year before. Joe Robbie did, though. Actually, he was pretty sore. His spanking-new National Football League franchise was bleeding money like a dolphin in the shark tank.

Well, old Joe was a pretty shrewd cookie who once ran for governor of South Dakota, became a prosecuting attorney, and convinced his old pal, Joe Foss, to give him a professional football franchise for seven million bucks he didn't even have.

But times were tough for old Joe right then. A lot of Miami high schools had better attendance at their Friday night games than the Dolphins got on Sunday. He knew that he needed a whole bunch of new players, plus a coach who knew how. And he needed them fast.

Fortunately, Robbie was able to steal Don Shula from the Baltimore Colts—which kept Colts owner Carroll Rosenbloom thoroughly pissed off until the day he drowned in the Atlantic Ocean behind his house in Golden Beach, Florida—to do the coaching.

General Manager Joe Thomas did the rest. He had grown up in Cortland, Ohio, just a few miles from where I did, and even though Joe had never been an exceptional athlete he had an uncanny ability to spot talent.

He drafted a bunch of "No-Name" college guys, and traded for Paul Warfield, Nick Buonoconti, and Marv Fleming. They took Miami to the playoffs in 1970, then the Super Bowl, and ultimately ran the table in 1972.

A new dynasty had been created.

I was thinking about dynasties, and greatness, this morning when I had Ghost and Heart out for a preseason conditioning run. It was eight o'clock and already oppressively hot. I was the only one who needed to sweat off some fat, but we all needed the legwork. Grouse season opens in a month.

As always, Ghost went first. The puppy howled and barked and carried on something awful while Ghost snuffled underneath the fiddlehead ferns and strained against the 40-foot lead. I watched her run, and whistled. If she heard me, she didn't heed me.

Not that she cared. Ghost ran as hard and as purposefully as she always has from Day One. Her nose was on the ground near the edge of a cedar swamp.

Even if she couldn't hear very well, or see where I was in the bright sunlight, it didn't stop her nose from working. She knew grouse were in there along the river. She'd been there before. A lot. And she by-God wanted more!

I watched Ghost quarter back and forth, and listened to Heart's frantic barking back at the truck. It reminded me of last year's final day of grouse season.

We weren't far from home. Actually, I was parked at the same spot where Ghost and I had our "Come to Jesus Meeting" several years before.

She was working the edge of some hummocks and tall viburnum bushes just a few minutes after getting on the ground when she locked. The grouse broke quickly, and I debated taking the shot. Then it was gone and Ghost was on the move again.

Moments later I heard the rhythmic beeping of the "point" mode on her collar and hurried forward. This time I never hesitated. The bird tipped over and Ghost had her end-of season grouse. We walked back to the truck. Elapsed time of hunt: ten minutes.

The shadows were setting and we were on the edge of Frenchman's Swamp. I was nervous. Would Heart run off into that tangled mess of bear and cat country?

Miraculously, I got through to Kate on my cell phone and told here where we were. "Do you want me to put *your* dog on the ground?"

Kate was quiet, thinking it over. Then she simply said "yes" and hung up.

I drove forward to where Ghost and I had stopped hunting, and loaded Heart's neck with all of the jewelry. Then he took off, and I held my breath. Back and forth. Back and forth. Looking, looking, hunting. He was whining with excitement.

When he stopped and stared at the base of a big old drooping cedar tree I barely had time to react before a grouse popped out into the clearing, heading right. As I raised the Beretta, another grouse flew left. My concentration evaporated. I shot at neither.

A third grouse went straight off into the swamp, unshootable, and number four flew over Heart's head and came into the wide open spaces on the edge of the trees.

Up came the shotgun. Click went the trigger.

When I got home and told Kate I had forgotten to reload when I swapped dogs, she slumped against the doorframe. A tear trickled down her cheek.

"After everything we went through with him the past two seasons, and you forgot to load the shotgun!" I could hear the unspoken "You Bonehead" in her voice.

"You're taking him to Wild Wings Game Farm tomorrow," Kate said. "He's not ending the season like *that*."

It was to be the turning point in Heart's education as a bird dog. I put a couple of chukkar out for Ghost, of course, but concentrated on the puppy. The more birds I put out, the steadier he became and the quicker he came roaring back to me when I whistled and called "Right Here!"

The boy even found a couple of pheasants that had survived some other folks' hunts, and he did a wonderful job of trailing and nailing.

A couple of weeks later we were back in Florida, and Kate insisted that We Three spend a day at Dream Lakes, letting the dogs have fun on quail.

Ghost always works first, befitting her stature in the hierarchy, and she'd covered the field and locked as solid as ever when her nose screamed "BIRD!"

It was obvious that her hearing and eyesight had deteriorated, but that didn't affect her determination. She ran and ran and ran until she found her birds. When the gun sounded, she found her birds yet again.

The look on her face with a bird cradled in her jaws was euphoric.

Heart, God bless him, was manic when I finally crated Ghost. He sniffed the dead quail and whined. I held out the bell and beeper, told him to sit, and he squirmed around like a hula dancer until I waved my arm forward.

He ran effortlessly. His big, deep chest sucked in air, and his tongue flopped. When I called "Right Here!" he raced back and skidded to a stop in front of me. His eyes glowed.

Two days later, I got a call from Gary Ashcroft. "The people at Cook's Sportland said you do some quail guiding?" Yes. "Got some time open next week?" Yes.

Heart was spectacular. He ran hard, came when called, found birds, and frantically chased one that Gary kept missing. When Heart finally rooted it out from under a muddy clump of roots in a filthy bog, and Gary killed it, everybody was ready for a cold drink and a soft place to sit down.

"That was some performance by both dogs," Gary said. "Ghost has the smarts, and Heart has the speed. I was really impressed."

So was I. But saddened, nonetheless, to see the passing of the torch. Just as I had been when Ghost took it from Ben. Just as I will be when Tug, the new puppy, takes it from Heart.

Don Schulz (standing) and Bill Ross share my enthusiasm for the beginning of yet another game dinner with this Opening Day grouse that Heart is jealously sniffing.

Chapter 26

Just Throw in a Little Dash of Salt...

A couple of other guys and I were spending the better part of a sweaty, bug-bit summer re-building a dilapidated old cabin 20 miles north of Grayling.

This was 30 years ago, and the idea of having our very own "camp" where we could hang out after a long day of hunting or fishing was mighty appealing. Cold beer, a hot meal, and a soft bed. Yep. That sounded pretty damn good.

The first time we saw "The Shack," as we came to call it, the door was off its hinges, and the old cabin's four tiny windows had been shot out. Tarpaper siding flapped piteously in the slightest breeze, and the roof leaked badly. Its only occupants during the previous 30 years had been ants, field mice, red squirrels, and maybe a stray porcupine.

The only redeeming value this dump had was the fact that it was nestled in about 30,000 acres of state land in the Deward Management Area. It also was just two good casts with a five-weight from the Manistee River.

It was going to cost us two hundred bucks a year to rent. We had to pay for all the fix-up materials, and no matter what we did to it, the place remained property of the legal owner. Which wasn't us.

Hell, you *know* we jumped at the chance to take the deal.

So now I'm back home in Lansing after a weekend of pounding nails while aching to toss a few flies at brookies in that enticing trout stream just outside the newly hung door. Wonderful. Except my guts are in a knot and I'm ready to puke.

"God," I moaned to Kate. "I'm never eating one more can of that glue they pass off as stew. I feel awful. *Please* give me a few decent recipes I can make on a three-burner Coleman stove!"

She shook her head, smiled, took a few minutes to scribble something on a piece of paper and handed it to me. "Try cooking this next weekend," she said.

My very first creation involved green peppers, sautéed onions, tomatoes, and half-inch-thick slices of cheap steak browned and served over rice. I still throw that together when I'm feeling nostalgic—or when the power goes out and I have to pull the camp stove off a shelf in the garage.

Thus began my culinary career.

Since it seemed that nobody I ran with back then either knew his way around a kitchen, or simply didn't want to handle the "chore," I became the designated camp cook for the Red Cedar Fly Fishers and Federation of Fly Fishers outings.

Actually, I didn't mind at all. For three reasons. First, I like to eat good food. Second, the rule is that the cook never cleans up—which means I could relax with a Scotch (or two) while other people were washing all of the dirty dishes, and scrubbing pots and skillets.

Third, I discovered that I really *like* to cook. It helps that I'm also pretty damned good at it!

Of course, I freely admit that my rapid progress as a cook largely was because of Kate. Not only did she pull out and show me countless skills from her enormous bag of cooking tricks, she played me like a fish.

Here's what happened.

She was working as a proofreader at the John Henry Company, just west of Lansing, which prints nearly all of the little tags that go into florist's pots. Her schedule was erratic. Depending upon deadlines, she often worked late into the evening.

One Tuesday, while I was in the middle of building a very dry martini, I decided to surprise her by having dinner ready when she got home sometime around eight. It was another one of those deadline nights.

"How wonderful!" Kate said when she walked into the aroma. Hell, I even had candles on the table. I don't recall if I had any "mood" music on the stereo. If I did, it would have been Kentucky bluegrass, because I clearly remember that I cooked fried chicken with mashed potatoes and homemade gravy.

"Oh, this is *delicious*," she said, setting the hook.

"Ummm, you can make this again anytime." Bzzzzzz—there goes the first run of line off the reel.

"The chicken is crusty, but still moist,"—ziiiing, a hundred yards of backing just evaporated.

Finally, "These are the best mashed potatoes I've ever eaten. So smooth and creamy. And the gravy is just perfect"—somebody reach for the gaff, 'cause I'm finished!

Actually, I was just beginning.

From then on I cooked at camp. I cooked at home. I cooked at *other* people's homes. It got to the point that I finally cobbled together my own personal cookbook in a three-ring-binder, and what I call my "camp kitchen"—a bag with a vast assortment of herbs and spices, a honing steel, Kershaw interchangeable-blade knife set, even a chef's apron.

And, yes, the "camp kitchen" is still operational. Just the other day it got me out of a jam because my "regular" kitchen was inexplicably out of Worcestershire sauce. Impossible, but true!

Naturally, I frequently put together a lunch of some kind when we take a break from chasing the dogs around North America during bird season. I already mentioned the Monte Cristo sandwiches I fixed for Don Schulz.

That would be French toast dusted with confectioner's sugar and served open-face with warm homemade blackberry sauce over thinly sliced ham and melted Swiss cheese.

"This is really *great*," Don said that afternoon. "I'll have to tell Charlie Mann to put this on the menu at Hunter's Creek Club."

I guess that got us started talking about birds and wild game and how some folks—including men—never appreciate the flavor of fowl or meat that didn't come packaged in Styrofoam and plastic wrap with a grocer's label glued to it.

"It's a shame," I told him. "I don't understand why people have this weird idea that something you personally kill out in the woods is somehow infested with vermin.

"For instance, I have a recipe that uses woodcock breast to make paté," I told Don. "It's got a bazillion calories, and a high enough cholesterol count to clog Hoover Dam. Kate makes French bread to go with it—baked from scratch on clay tiles in the oven— and it's to die for.

"I mean, it's every bit as good—if not far better—than paté I've eaten in any restaurant, including Brennan's in New Orleans. And the venison fillets with Béarnaise sauce that I make for a main course are fantastic.

"That's because I do a slow and really careful job when I butcher my deer. Even the women think it's aged prime beef. And I don't tell 'em any different."

"That," Don said with a dreamy expression on his face, "sounds delicious!"

"Tell you what, how about you and Bill Ross coming over in a couple of weeks—that would be November 8—and I'll make that pate and some sort of dinner?"

As it turned out, the only thing Schulz and Ross were able to eat that particular day was crow. They'd called to beg off dinner at our house in order to be part of a crazed mass of 112,118 football fans who watched Ohio State beat their Michigan State Spartans 33-23.

Ten days later, they were still in agony as they shoveled down Kate's marvelous French bread spread lavishly with woodcock paté. But a new tradition had begun. Now the first Saturday in November—no matter who's on the football schedule—is reserved for the wild game dinner.

Our cast of characters has swelled—and changed—over the years. Jackie Norcross became a fixture (except when she's back in France with her family). Rex Farver and John David Korte usually are here. So is Jim Powers.

Recently, we added Eric and Susan Sharp, Doug and Sherrie Fairbanks, Dave and Sue Smethhurst, and Bob and Mary Slezek. Paul and Judy Mesack, and Bruce and Bea Patrick were back with us. Rex, JD and Victor Edwards didn't make it, but Lansing Contingent of Dennis Pace, Anne Grofvert, Jack Helder and Zabby Cox contributed plenty of food and laughter.

The "body count" got up to 23 last year, so we brought in the table and chairs from the porch and borrowed more from Victor. Fortunately, the dining room's 12 by 24 feet, so we managed just fine. Except for one of the porch chairs that started to ever-so-slowly sway underneath Dave Smethurst.

When he ended up getting dumped unceremoniously onto the floor, Kate was aghast. I winced, because she had *told* me not to use that chair and I just knew I'd catch hell later (deservedly so, I've gotta admit). Everybody else was very quiet. Except Dave. Who laughed like hell.

I don't remember which course we'd just eaten. For all I know we might well have been finishing up the myriad bottles of wine everybody'd brought, or were sipping my home-brew Hunter's Hearth Liquor.

Game Dinner nights tend to be like that. Lots of stories about spectacular dog work, crazy-wild birds that flew like F-15s, pitiful excuses for shots that only killed leaves, and an awful lot of belt-loosening. I'm in a real dilemma, though. It's nearly time for this year's feast and I still haven't decided on the menu.

Except for the woodcock paté. *That's* a constant! It's what got this whole affair started, and it simply wouldn't be the game dinner without paté. It is, after all, the culmination of that glorious communion of men and their dogs—a fine and fitting way for all of us to remember, ultimately, that being out in the woods is really about friendship.

And all of those wonderful bird dogs that make our lives complete.

Ghost put on a fine display from Mike Chirappa.

A delicious beginning for a delicious meal.

CHAPTER 27

SAVORING THE HARVEST: RECIPES FROM OUR ANNUAL GAME DINNER

APPETIZERS

CAPT. TONY'S WOODCOCK PÂTÉ

INGREDIENTS

13	woodcock breast
3	sticks butter
3	thin onion slices
2	bay leaves
¼ cup	sweet sherry
¼ cup	brandy
salt to taste	

PREPARATION

Cut woodcock breasts into even size pieces. Melt one stick butter in skillet, while allowing remaining two sticks to soften. Sauté onion slices until soft. Add bay leaves, sherry, salt, and woodcock. Cook until browned. Discard bay leaves and puree in blender, adding small chunks of butter and brandy until the mixture is smooth.

Pour into muffin tin to make individual servings, and refrigerate overnight. Serve with KATE'S TILE-BAKED FRENCH BREAD (see page 176).

KATE'S TILE-BAKED FRENCH BREAD

INGREDIENTS

4 ½ tsp	yeast
2 ½ cups	warm water
6 cups	bread flour
2 tsp	salt
2 tsp	water

PREPARATION

Sprinkle yeast over water in large bowl. Allow to "bloom" (about 5 min.). Add 3 cups flour ½ cup at a time, beating with electric mixer about 10 min. Disolve salt in water, and blend in. Stir in remaining flour, then knead on floured cloth 8 min.

Grease a large bowl and place dough in it. Place plastic wrap on top of dough and let rise 2 hours at room temperature. Then punch down dough, briefly knead in bowl, then re-cover and rise again 1 ½ hours.

Remove rack from oven; place place clay tiles on it. Sprinkle tiles with cornmeal, (greased cookie sheets can be used instead.) Separate dough into 4 pieces and shape each by hand into a 16-inch length. Place on tiles. Cover with a cloth; let rise until doubled in size.

Place shallow pan on lowesst ov en rack. Preheat oven to 450°F. Carefully add 1 cup water to pan to create steam, Cut several 1/4 inch slashes into dough. Bake loaves on middle rack 25 minutes or until golden brown. Remove to wire rack to cool.

HUNTER'S CREEK CLUB SMOKED PHEASANT

INGREDIENTS

2	whole pheasant, plucked & dressed
2 gal	water
1 cup	salt
1 cup	brown sugar
	hickory wood chips

PREPARATION

Soak the pheasant overnight in the water/salt/sugar solution. Pat dry and smoke 3 to 4 hours over moistened wood chips. Slice into serving pieces.

CRABMEAT HUSHPUPPIES
WITH REMOULADE SAUCE

INGREDIENTS

1 cup	cooked crabmeat, rinsed
1½ cups	milk
1½ cups	flour
2	eggs, beaten
1 tsp	baking soda
3 Tbsp	butter
¼ cup	green bell pepper, minced
¼ cup	scallion greens and bulbs, minced
1 Tbsp	garlic, minced
1½ Tbsp	Cajun seasoning
1 tsp	salt
1 tsp	ground black pepper
4 cups	cooking oil

PREPARATION

Bring the oil to high heat in a 4qt pot but do not boil. Meanwhile, melt the butter in a skillet and sauté the pepper, scallions, and garlic until just soft. Add the crab and mix well. Remove from heat.

Mix the flour, baking soda and seasonings in a large bowl. Add the crab mixture, milk and eggs to create a batter. Use a large spoon and spatula to carefully ease 3 or 4 hushpuppies into the hot oil. Cook until golden, drain on paper towels. Serve with Remoulade Sauce (see recipe on page 191).

SCALLOP-STUFFED MUSHROOMS

INGREDIENTS

10	mushrooms (jumbo-sized)
1 stick	butter
2 Tbsp	sweet onion, minced
3 cups	fresh breadcrumbs
1 Tbsp	dried tarragon
¾ lb	bay scallops, minced
	salt & pepper to taste
1 cup	Parmesan cheese, grated

parsley, lemon wedges & cherry tomatoes for garnish

PREPARATION

Melt butter in large skillet and sauté minced onion until soft. Meanwhile, remove stems from mushrooms, mince and add to onion. Add breadcrumbs, tarragon, scallops, salt, and pepper. Mix well and heat until just warm.

Place mushroom caps on shallow baking dish and stuff with mixture. Bake 20 minutes in preheated 350°F oven, then sprinkle with parmesan and broil until light brown.

SMOKED SALMON

INGREDIENTS

1	salmon, filleted
4 gal	water
1½ cups	salt
2 sticks	butter
2 tsp	curry powder
1 tsp	salt
½ tsp	black pepper
2	limes, sliced
1	lemon, sliced

PREPARATION

Soak salmon overnight in saltwater.

Cover heavy cookie sheet with thin slices of lemon and lime. Pat salmon dry with paper towel and place skin side down on citris. Melt butter and add curry, salt, and pepper. Pour butter mix over salmon.

Place soaked alderwood chips on very hot charcoal fire in a closed grill and smoke salmon until flesh flakes with a fork. Remove meat from skin and bones; serve with water biscuits or hot crusty bread.

RUMAKI

INGREDIENTS

8 ounce can	whole water chestnuts*
2 Tbsp	lemon juice
1 Tbsp	Worcestershire sauce
1 Tbsp	seasoned salt
½ lb.	bacon
wooden toothpicks	

PREPARATION

Thoroughly mix ingredients and marinate 10 minutes. Wrap each water chestnut with a slice of bacon and secure with toothpick. Broil until bacon is crisp, turn and finish broiling. 00

SOUP COURSE

CREAM OF ASPARAGUS

INGREDIENTS

2 lb	asparagus
6 Tbsp	butter
4 Tbsp	flour
3	thin onion slices
1 Tbsp	salt
1 tsp	pepper
2 cups	chicken broth
2 cups	milk00
paprika	

PREPARATION

Sauté onion slices in 4 Tbsp melted butter, then remove with slotted spoon. In blender, liquefy asparagus in broth, adding sautéed onion, then strain through cheesecloth to eliminate pulp.

Meanwhile, melt remaining 2 Tbsp butter and add flour, stirring to a froth. Slowly add asparagus liquid, stirring constantly, then add milk and seasonings and top each serving bowl with paprika.

Grandma Lucy's Minestrone

BROTH INGREDIENTS

4-5 lbs	stock meat & bones
enough water to cover stock meat	
6	carrots
2	onions, quartered
6	celery stalks with leaves
4	bay leaves
1 Tbsp	peppercorns
2 Tbsp each	dried basil, oregano

PREPARATION

Mix all ingredients in large stock pot. Bring to a boil and cook until the meat is tender. Reserve broth. Shred meat from bones and reserve. Discard bones and remaining ingredients.

SOUP INGREDIENTS

1 lb	bacon
½ cup	olive oil
2	medium onions, chopped
4	carrots, julienned
5 cloves	minced garlic
2 each	green & yellow zucchini skins, julienned
¼ head	cabbage, cored and shredded
30 oz.	diced peeled tomatoes
1 Tbsp each	oregano, basil, salt, black pepper
1 box	orzo pasta

2 cans	cannellini (white) beans
1 lb	fresh green beans
½ cup	freshly grated Parmesan cheese

Fry cubed bacon in another large pot until crisp and remove with slotted spoon. Heat oil and sauté onion until soft. Add garlic, carrots and zucchini. Season with basil, oregano, salt and pepper. Cover and simmer, stirring occasionally, until veggies are soft.

Add cabbage and cook uncovered, stirring until wilted. Pour in reserved broth and shredded meat. Add tomatoes and pasta, boiling until pasta is swollen and soft.

Add beans and parmesan and adjust salt to taste. Serve with more grated Parmesan over the top of each serving bowl.

CRAB NEWBURG

INGREDIENTS

2 cups	crabmeat, rinsed
½ stick	butter
¼ cup	vermouth
3	egg yolks
1 cup	heavy cream
rice	(per package directions) or toast points

PREPARATION

Melt the butter in a pan and stir in crabmeat. Add vermouth and cook 3 minutes. Meanwhile, whisk egg yolks in the top half of a double boiler. Add cream and crab. Cook, stirring constantly, until mixture thickens. Serve over rice or toast.

VICHYSSOISE

INGREDIENTS

6 cups	chicken broth
3 ½ cups	potatoes, peeled & sliced
3 cups	wild onion or leeks, sliced
1 tsp	salt
1 cup	heavy cream or half & half
1/8 tsp	white pepper
3 Tbsp	chopped chives

PREPARATION

Cook broth, potatoes, onion and salt over medium-low heat 50 minutes. Puree in blender until smooth, then stir in cream. Season with pepper, and salt to taste. Chill until very cold. Top each serving with chives.

CAPT. TONY'S CHOWDER

INGREDIENTS

2	trout, skinned & boned
2 Tbsp	olive oil
1 cup	bacon, cooked & diced
1	onion, finely chopped
2	garlic cloves, minced
½ cup	green bell pepper, diced
½ cup	red bell pepper, diced
3	red potatoes, boiled & diced
2 qt	half & half
1½ Tbsp	basil, chopped

salt & pepper to taste

PREPARATION

Boil the potatoes in a large pot. Remove to a bowl and poach the trout in the same water 5 minutes. Remove trout and reserve the liquid.

In a separate skillet, fry the bacon until nearly crisp. Add olive oil, onion, peppers, and garlic. Sauté until soft. Season with salt, pepper and basil. Add the potatoes, chunks of fish, and half & half. Add reserved liquid if necessary to cover ingredients by one inch. Stir constantly to avoid scorching. Do not bring to a boil. Serve with Kate's TILED-BAKED FRENCH BREAD (PAGE 176).

CAPT. TONY'S CRABCAKES

INGREDIENTS

3 cups	freshly picked crabmeat
¼ cup	clarified butter
1 cup	fresh breadcrumbs
2	eggs, beaten
½ tsp	white pepper
½ tsp	salt
2 tsp	Dijon mustard
1 Tbsp	Worcestershire sauce
2 Tbsp	minced parsley
⅔ cups	mayonnaise
1 Tbsp	dried tarragon
1 tsp	Tabasco sauce
3 Tbsp	Crisco or olive oil

PREPARATION

Break off the crab claws and refrigerate. Serve with clarified butter while finishing the crabcakes.

Remove the carapace from the underside of the crabs and begin "picking" the meat after discarding the yellowish "innards."

Rinse the "pickings" in cold water and chop coarsely. Mix all ingredients except oil and shape into ½-inch thick patties the size of a hamburger. Heat the oil until smoky hot and fry the crabcakes 3-5 minutes each side or until lightly browned.

FISH COURSE

CHINOOK SALMON WITH DILL STUFFING

INGREDIENTS

4	salmon fillets, skinned
3 Tbsp	butter, melted
salt and pepper to taste	

STUFFING

2 cups	fresh breadcrumbs, finely crumbled
2 Tbsp	onion, minced
½ cup	dill pickle, minced
1 tsp	dried sage
½ tsp	dried thyme
6 Tbsp	butter, melted
½ cup	cream
2 Tbsp	dill pickle juice
salt and pepper to taste	

PREPARATION

Skin the fish and rinse under cold water. Pat dry and lightly pound fillets between wax paper to an even thickness of ¼-inch. Salt and pepper fillets, and cut into 1½-inch-wide medallions.

Mix stuffing ingredients thoroughly and spread it onto the medallions. Roll up each and skewer with toothpicks. Drizzle the reserved 3 Tbsp butter over the medallions, cover. Bake 30 minutes at 375°F, uncovering for the final 10 minutes.

TROUT HEMINGWAY WITH REMOULADE SAUCE

INGREDIENTS

4	whole trout, dressed
2	green onions, chopped
1½ Tbsp	parsley, chopped
1 Tbsp	lemon juice
¼ tsp	white pepper
½ Tbsp	salt
4	bacon strips, thick-sliced
1 cup	flour
2 Tbsp	butter, broken into small chunks
¼ cup	cornmeal

Combine onion, parsley, lemon juice and pepper. Sprinkle trout cavities with salt, then spread each with onion mixture.

Dredge trout exteriors with flour and butter, then cornmeal.

Meanwhile, fry bacon in large skillet until crisp. Remove bacon and cook trout in bacon drippings until they "puff," turning once (about 5 minutes per side). Insert one slice of bacon into trout. Top with Remoulade Sauce (see recipe on page 191).

REMOULADE SAUCE

2	roasted red peppers, peeled
1 cup	mayonnaise
¼ cup	parsley, chopped
1	green onion, minced
1Tbsp	lemon rind, grated
1½Tbsp	horseradish
1Tbsp	capers, drained
¼tsp	salt & pepper

PREPARATION

Core, seed and rinse peppers. Flatten on roasting pan and broil until outer skin is charred black. Remove peppers to paper bag and allow skin to steam loose. When cool enough to handle, peel off and discard charred skin, add peppers to the the mayonnaise and blend in food processor until smooth. Add remaining ingredients and process until smooth. Chill 30 minutes.

SHRIMP CALABRESE

INGREDIENTS

12	large shrimp, peeled
½ cup	crabmeat
1 cup	fresh breadcrumbs
½ cup	salted crackers, crushed
½ cup	parsley, chopped
4 Tbsp	butter, melted
½ cup	Parmesan, grated
1 Tbsp	lemon juice
¼ tsp	Tabasco
1 clove	garlic, minced
¼ tsp	tarragon
	salt and pepper, to taste
3 Tbsp	olive oil

PREPARATION

Butterfly each shrimp. Mix crab, bread, crackers, parsley, parmesan, lemon juice, tarragon, salt/pepper and Tabasco. Lightly sauté garlic in butter and add crab mix, stirring well.

Stuff each shrimp and nest together on baking sheet. Drizzle olive oil over shrimp and bake 15 minutes in preheated 400°F oven.

George Washington's Bass Roast

INGREDIENTS

4	sea bass fillets
5 Tbsp	olive oil
2 cup	leeks, whites only, sliced thinly
3 cup	potatoes, peeled, sliced thinly
3 Tbsp	balsamic vinegar
¾ cup	heavy cream
¾ cup	walnuts, chopped and lightly roasted

salt and pepper to taste

PREPARATION

Skin the bass fillets, then cut into 2-inch squares. Heat the olive oil in a skillet and sauté the leeks, 10 minutes until wilted. Reserve olive oil drippings.

Arrange the potatoes on the bottom of a roasting pan, then the leeks and finally the bass.

Combine the reserved oil, vinegar, and cream. Whisk vigorously. Add salt and pepper and pour over the fish. Bake 10 minutes in preheated 450°F degree oven.

Sprinkle with roasted walnuts.

STUFFED STEELHEAD WITH WHITE SAUCE

INGREDIENTS

3-4 lbs	steelhead, skinned and filleted
2 cups	cooked wild rice (see page 209)
2 Tbsp	almonds, finely chopped
2 Tbsp	Parmesan cheese, grated
1 Tbsp	parsley, chopped
1 Tbsp	lemon juice
1 tsp	grated orange peel
	salt and pepper to taste

WHITE SAUCE

INGREDIENTS

4 Tbsp	butter
4 Tbsp	flour
½ tsp	salt
½ tsp	white pepper
2 cups	milk

PREPARATION

Melt butter and stir in flour until mixture froths. Slowly pour in milk, stirring constantly, until it's the consistency of honey. Season with salt and pepper. Set aside.

Pound fillets gently between waxed paper and cut into serving sizes. Sprinkle with lemon juice and orange peel, then spoon wild rice onto each slice of fish. Roll and secure with a toothpick. Place fish into baking dish, spoon white sauce over all, and sprinkle with Parmesan, almonds, and parsley. Bake in preheated 350°F oven 30 minutes.

FOWL COURSE

GROUSE CORDON BLEU WITH MORNAY SAUCE

INGREDIENTS

2	grouse breasts
3 Tbsp	olive oil
½ cup	diced mushrooms
¼ cup	diced red bell pepper
1 Tbsp	diced shallots
¼ tsp	dried tarragon
4 thin slices	Provolone or Swiss cheese
4 thin slices	Prosciutto ham
½ tsp	salt
8 strips	bacon

PREPARATION

Bone grouse breasts into halves, pound lightly to ¼ -inch thickness between wax paper, and sprinkle with salt. Meanwhile, heat oil and sauté mushrooms, red pepper, shallots, and tarragon. Spread mixture on breast halves, then place one slice each ham and cheese on breast half. Roll up and wrap each with 2 slices bacon. Skewer with toothpicks and bake 30 minutes in preheated 350°F oven. Finish frying bacon in skillet. To serve, spoon Mornay Sauce over grouse breasts and crumble bacon over all.

MORNAY SAUCE

INGREDIENTS

2 Tbsp	butter
½ cup	chicken broth
½ tsp	salt
½ cup	grated Parmesan
2 Tbsp	flour
½ cup	half & half
1/8 tsp	cayenne pepper
1/8 tsp	white pepper
1/8 tsp	nutmeg

PREPARATION

Melt butter over low heat and stir in flour until mixture froths. Slowly stir in broth and cream. Bring to a boil, stirring to consistency of warm honey. Boil 1 minute and add seasonings. Serve over grouse.

GROUSE RAPHAEL WEILL

INGREDIENTS

2	breasts, halved
¼ cup	butter
18 ozs	artichoke hearts
6 tsp	minced shallots
½ lb	mushrooms, sliced
3 tsp	chopped chives
2½ cups	half and half
¼ cup	sherry
¼ cup	chicken broth
3 Tbsp	flour
¼ tsp	salt
1/8 tsp	pepper

PREPARATION

Season breast halves with salt and pepper, then lightly brown in melted butter and remove with slotted spatula. Sauté shallots 1 minute. Add artichokes, mushrooms, chives, cream and sherry. Cover and cook 25 minute on low heat.

Remove grouse to warm platter. Shake flour and broth in small jar until blended and gradually add to skillet. Stir over medium-low heat until mixture thickens. Return grouse to skillet and heat 2 minutes. Serve over wide egg noodles that have been lightly buttered and salted.

GROUSE WITH WILD BLACKBERRY SAUCE

INGREDIENTS

1	whole grouse, skin on
2 Tbsp	olive oil
¼ tsp	salt
⅛ tsp	pepper
4 leaves	fresh rosemary

PREPARATION

Sprinkle salt and pepper inside cavity of the bird and insert rosemary. Brush grouse with oil and roast 15 minutes in preheated 425°F oven, or until juices run clear.

BLACKBERRY SAUCE

INGREDIENTS

1 cup	blackberries
½ cup	sugar
1 Tbsp	cornstarch
½ cup	water

PREPARATION

Heat sugar, cornstarch, and water over medium heat and boil 2 minutes. Stir in berries and bring to a boil. Simmer over low heat 5 minute. Spoon over plated grouse pieces.

Hunter's Creek Pheasant

WITH SHOTGUN SAUCE AND RICE CASSEROLE

INGREDIENTS

1	pheasant, halved lengthwise
4	slices bacon
	salt & pepper
1 Tbsp	butter
1 Tbsp	currant jelly
1	large onion slice

PREPARATION

Place heavy aluminum foil on cookie sheet. Lay 2 slices bacon on foil, then one pheasant half. Salt & pepper to taste, then place butter, jelly and onion slice on pheasant. Set remaining pheasant on top, then cover with bacon and wrap the foil tightly. Bake 1 hour in preheated 350°F oven.

Open foil and spoon some Shotgun Sauce over bird. Broil until light brown, turn bird, spoon on more sauce and brown. Serve with remaining sauce.

Shotgun Sauce

INGREDIENTS

1 cup	currant jelly
½ cup	butter
1 tsp	Worcestershire sauce
1 Tbsp	bourbon

PREPARATION

Mix ingredients and boil 5 minutes. Stir and remove foam.

Keep sauce on low heat until ready to serve to prevent carmelizing.

Rice Casserole

INGREDIENTS

1¼ cup	brown rice
1¼ cup	butter
2	stalks celery, chopped
1	medium onion, chopped
½ cup each	green & red pepper, chopped
½ cup	sliced mushrooms
1½ cup	chicken broth

PREPARATION

Sauté rice in butter until slightly softened. Mix all ingredients in 3qt. casserole dish and bake 1½ hours. at 350°F. Toss lightly and serve with pheasant on top.

BRAISED DUCK WITH CHERRIES

INGREDIENTS

5 to 6 lb	duck
¼ cup	bacon fat
1 Tbsp	minced shallot
1 ½ cup	red wine
½ tsp	salt
1	bay leaf
$1/_8$ tsp	marjoram
2 Tbsp	cornstarch
1 cup	flour
1 can	pitted black cherries

PREPARATION

Cut duck into quarters, dredge in flour and braise in bacon fat. Remove to warm plate. Sauté shallot 1 minute. Add wine, salt, bay leaf and marjoram. Heat over medium and boil 1 minute.

Drain cherries. Add cornstarch to cherry juice and bring to boil, stirring constantly. Reduce heat to low. Add cherries; heat through and pour over duck.

MEAT COURSE

VENISON FILET WITH BÉARNAISE SAUCE

INGREDIENTS

4	inch-thick fillets
2 Tbsp	Kitchen Bouquet
salt & pepper	

PREPARATION

Brush venison with Kitchen Bouquet, season, and grill over medium-high heat 5 minutes per side for medium-rare.

BÉARNAISE SAUCE

INGREDIENTS

2	egg yolks
2 Tbsp	lemon juice
2 sticks	butter (cold)
1Tbsp	minced shallot
1 tsp	tarragon
½ tsp	chervil
2 Tbsp	white wine

PREPARATION

Whisk lemon juice into egg yolks over low heat. Add shallot, tarragon, chervil, wine and 1 stick butter (keep the other stick in the refrigerator. Stir constantly with wooden spoon (a metal spoon generates too much heat) until butter is melted. Stir in second stick of butter, which has remained refrigerated, until melted.

VENISON ROAST À LA BENNETT

INGREDIENTS

3 lb	venison roast
2 bottles	premium beer
3 Tbsp	Kitchen Bouquet
4 Tbsp	bacon fat
4 Tbsp	butter
4 Tbsp	sherry
	salt & pepper

PREPARATION

Marinate venison overnight in beer. Then brush with Kitchen Bouquet and sprinkle with salt & pepper. Make deep cuts into roast with a sharp knife and insert pieces of butter and bacon fat.

Roast 1½ hour in preheated 350°F oven, basting frequently. Add sherry during last 10 minutes of roasting and continue basting. Slice very thinly against the grain and quickly heat slices in basting juices.

VENISON TERIYAKI

INGREDIENTS

3 lb	venison steaks
¾ cup	canola oil
¼ cup	soy sauce
¼ cup	honey
2 Tbsp	cider vinegar
2 Tbsp	chopped onion
1 clove	minced garlic
1½ tsp	ground ginger

Mix all ingredients and marinate 24 hours. Grill over medium heat 3-5 min. per side depending upon thickness of steaks.

FARVER'S ELK TENDERLOIN

INGREDIENTS

1	elk tenderloin
1/3 cup	chopped onion
1/3 cup	lemon juice
1/3 cup	bourbon
1 Tbsp	honey
1 Tbsp	soy sauce
½ Tbsp	ground ginger
1 Tbsp	olive oil
2 cloves	minced garlic
¼ tsp	salt
1/8 tsp	pepper

PREPARATION

Mix all ingredients, reserving ¼-cup of marinade fro gravy. Marinate elk 4 hours, then roast 40 minutes in preheated oven at 350°F.

GRAVY

Melt 2 Tbsp each butter and bacon fat. Stir in 4 Tbsp flour. Slowly add reserved marinate, stirring to desired consistency. Boil for 1 minute.

ELK STEAKS DIANE

INGREDIENTS

4	elk steaks
1 stick	butter
1 cup	sliced mushrooms
4 Tbsp	minced shallot
1 clove	minced garlic
¼ tsp	salt
2 tsp	lemon juice
2 tsp	Worcestershire sauce
4 Tbsp	parsley
4 Tbsp	butter
2 Tbsp	sherry

PREPARATION

Melt 1 stick butter in heavy skillet. Sauté mushrooms, shallots, garlic, salt, lemon juice, and Worcestershire. Stir in parsley, and remove to warm platter with slotted spoon.

Melt remaining 4 Tbsp butter over medium-high heat, then add sherry. Sear steaks 4 minutes. Turn and cook additional 4 minutes. Serve topped with sauce.

SIDE DISHES

WILD RICE

INGREDIENTS

1 cup	wild rice
2½ cups	water
2 cubes	chicken bouillon
4 Tbsp	butter, halved
1	sweet onion, chopped
1 cup	mushrooms, chopped
	salt to taste

PREPARATION

Melt 2 Tbsp butter in skillet and sauté onions over medium-low heat. Stir in mushrooms and onion, turn heat to low, cover. Meanwhile, melt 2 Tbsp butter in large sauce pan and sauté wild rice over medium heat 3 minutes.

Add water and bouillon, increase heat to high, and boil rice until water is absorbed and small craters form on the surface. Stir in mushrooms and onion mixture, cover and simmer 30 minutes.

HONEY-GLAZED CARROTS

INGREDIENTS

½ lb	carrot rounds
3 Tbsp	butter
1½ Tbsp	seasoned salt
2 Tbsp	minced chives

PREPARATION

Bring water to a rolling boil and cook carrot rounds about 3 minutes, or until soft but still crisp. Drain, add softened butter, seasoned salt and chives. Stir together well.

RED POTATOES WITH BUTTER & PARSLEY

INGREDIENTS

½ lb	small red potatoes
3 Tbsp	butter
½ tsp	salt
3 Tbsp	chopped parsley

PREPARATION

Bring water to a rolling boil and cook potatoes about 10 minutes, or until soft but not mushy. Drain, add butter, salt and parsley.

GRILLED ASPARAGUS PARMESAN

INGREDIENTS

½ lb	asparagus tips
2 Tbsp	olive oil
½ tsp	cayenne pepper
½ cup	grated parmesan
	salt to taste

PREPARATION

Snap asparagus spears and place tips on metal broiling pan (freeze the butts until you have enough to make cream of asparagus soup—do the same with broccoli). Dribble oil over spears, season with salt and cayenne, top with grated parmesan. Bake 6 minutes in preheated 425 °F oven.

GOLDEN RICE

INGREDIENTS

1 cup	long grin rice
2½ cups	water
2	chicken bouillon cubes
1½ tsp	turmeric
	salt to taste

PREPARATION

Add bouillon to water and bring to a rolling boil. Add rinsed rice and cook until water is mostly absorbed and tiny craters appear on the surface. Turn the heat to low, cover tightly, and simmer 30 minutes. Fluff rice with a fork and sprinkle in salt and turmeric, stirring well.

BUTTERED EGG NOODLES WITH TARRAGON

INGREDIENTS

½ lb	wide egg noodles
3 Tbsp	butter
1 tsp	dried tarragon flakes
salt to taste	

PREPARATION

Boil noodles until soft, but still firm. Drain and mix in softened butter, salt, and tarragon. Stir well.

CALCUTTA CAYENNE COB CORN

INGREDIENTS

4 ears	husked corn
2 Tbsp	cayenne pepper
2 tsp	salt
2	limes

PREPARATION

Bring water to rolling boil in large pot and immerse corn for 3 minutes before draining. Mix salt/cayenne mixture in individual serving dishes. Cut limes in half and rub cut side in salt/cayenne then rub onto corn.

BROCCOLI WITH CHEESE SAUCE

INGREDIENTS

½ lb	broccoli florets
2 Tbsp	butter
2 Tbsp	flour
¼ tsp	salt
$1/_8$ tsp	pepper
1 cup	milk
8 oz	shredded Cheddar cheese

PREPARATION

Trim the broccoli and steam the florets until softened but still crisp (freeze the st0ems until you have enough to make cream of broccoli soup--see Cream of Asparagus Soup on page 182). Melt the butter, then stir in flour and stir until mixture froths. Add salt and pepper, and slowly pour in milk, stirring constantly. Add cheese and stir until melted.

Twice-Baked Potatoes

INGREDIENTS

4 medium	baking potatoes
2 Tbsp	butter
2 Tbsp	heavy cream
½ tsp	salt
½ tsp	pepper
4 oz	grated Cheddar cheese
½ cup	grated Parmesan

PREPARATION

Bake potatoes in preheated 400°F oven 30 minutes. Scoop meat into mixing bowl, reserving skins. Add remaining ingredients except Parmesan and whip until smooth with mixer. Adjust as needed with additional butter, cream and salt to make a creamy filling. Refill skins with mixture, top with parmesan and broil until cheese is lightly browned.

SALADS

HELDER'S AVOCADO/RASPBERRY SALAD

INGREDIENTS

4 cups	mixed greens
2	green onions, sliced
½ cup	walnuts
2	avocados in ½-inch chunks
1 cup	raspberries and/or blueberries
4-5	pitted Kalamata olives per serving
½ cup	red wine & vinegar dressing
	or pomegranate dressing
1 cup	ground Reggiano Parmesan

Pepper to taste

No Salt. Pitted Kalamata olives are salty enough

PREPARATION

Mix ingredients, then add dressing. Top each serving with Parmesan.

ROSS' RED DOG SLAW

INGREDIENTS

1 head	shredded green cabbage
1	sweet onion, minced
1	carrot, grated
½ cup	parsley, chopped
1 cup	white vinegar
½ cup	sugar
1½ tsp	celery seed
1½ tsp	salt
1½ tsp	dry mustard
1 cup	canola oil

PREPARATION

In a large bowl, mix cabbage, onion, carrot & parsley.

In sauce pan, bring vinegar, sugar, celery seed, salt & mustard to a boil. Add oil and return to boil, stirring constantly. Remove from heat and pour over cabbage. Refrigerate overnight. Drain off excess dressing, toss well, and serve.

KATE'S ARTICHOKE SALAD

INGREDIENTS

2 cans	quartered artichoke hearts
1 can	jumbo black olives, halved
4	ripe tomatoes, cut in eighths
1 cup	mild pepper rings
1 cup	coarsely chopped red pepper
1 cup	coarsely chopped green pepper

Italian dressing

PREPARATION

Drain artichokes and olives. Mix everything and allow to marinate four hours before serving.

BALSAMIC TOMATOES

INGREDIENTS

4	ripe tomatoes
2 Tbsp	balsamic vinegar
1 Tbsp	olive oil
½ tsp	salt
¼ tsp	thyme

PREPARATION

Slice tomatoes and marinate 30 minutes in vinegar, oil and salt at room temperature. Sprinkle with thyme when serving.

Desserts

Raspberry-Fudge Brownies

Makes one 8-inch pan; the recipe doubles easily. It's best to start this early in the day, or the day before you want to serve them, because the brownies have to be completely cool before you glaze them. These are very rich and also very dense because there's no baking powder or baking soda in them.

BROWNIES

3 squares	unsweetened baking chocolate
½ cup	shortening
3	eggs
1½ cups	granulated sugar
1½ tsp	vanilla
¼ tsp	salt
1 cup	flour
1 cup	chopped walnuts
1 cup	raspberry jam

FUDGE GLAZE

1 square	unsweetened baking chocolate
2 Tbsp	butter
2 Tbsp	light corn syrup
1 cup	powdered sugar
1 Tbsp	milk
1 tsp	vanilla

Grease 8-inch square pan. Preheat oven to 325°F for glass or dark metal pan; 350°F for shiny metal. Melt chocolate with shortening; cool slightly.

In a large bowl, blend together eggs, sugar, vanilla, and salt. Stir in chocolate mixture, then flour. Fold in chopped nuts. Turn out into well-greased 8-inch pan. Bake about 40 minutes, until toothpick inserted in middle comes out with just a few crumbs attached.

Spoon jam over hot brownies; spread carefully. (Some of the brownie crust might get mixed in with it; that's okay.) Let cool completely.

To make glaze: Melt the chocolate and butter together. Blend in light corn syrup. Stir in powdered sugar, milk, and vanilla; mix well. Carefully spread over the cooled brownies. If some of the jam gets mixed in with it, just smooth it over. If desired, top with more walnuts.

Apple-Cranberry Shortcake

INGREDIENTS

4 cups	thinly sliced peeled apples
1 cup	fresh cranberries
¼ cup	water
⅔ cup	packed brown sugar
½ tsp	cinnamon
¼ tsp	salt

Bring to a boil; cover and simmer until apples are tender. Spoon over shortcakes.

SHORTCAKE

2 cup	flour
2 Tbsp	sugar
3 tsp	baking powder
1 tsp	salt
⅓ cup	Crisco
1 cup	milk

Heat oven to 450°F. Mix dry ingredients; cut in shortening until mix has a texture like fine meal. Stir in milk until just spoonable. Pat into greased cake pan and bake 15-20 minutes.

KATE'S ORGASM BARS

INGREDIENTS

¾ cup	butter, softened
¾ cup	confectioners sugar
1½ cup	flour
2	eggs
1 cup	packed brown sugar
2 Tbsp	flour
½ tsp	baking powder
½ tsp	salt
½ tsp	vanilla
1 cup	chopped pecans

PREPARATION

Preheat over to 350°F.

Whip butter and confectioners sugar until creamy. Blend in flour and press mixture into ungreased 13x9x2 baking pan. Bake 13 minutes. Mix remaining ingredients. Spread over baked layer and bake another 20 minutes. Cool before serving.

Ghost nails a woodcock on yet another classic October morning.

BLACKBERRY PIE

FILLING INGREDIENTS

6 cups	fresh blackberries
2 cups	sugar
5 Tbsp	tapioca
2 Tbsp	softened butter, cut into chunks

CRUST INGREDIENTS

$2^2/_3$ cups	flour
1 tsp	salt
1 cup	Crisco, divided
1 cup	ice water

PREPARATION

Mix berries, sugar and tapioca, set aside. In a separate bowl, mix salt and flour, then cut in ½ cup Crisco until mixture has a fine texture. Cut in remaining Crisco, then add 6 Tbsp ice water and stir well. If flour doesn't "clean" bowl, gradually add more ice water. Divide mixture and roll out bottom crust on pastry cloth. Roll up cloth, then unroll crust into 9-inch pie plate.

Fill with berry mixture and top with butter chunks. Roll out top crust and pinch edges together. Make three slashes in top crust with sharp knife, then cover edges with aluminum foil. Bake 25 min. in preheated 425°F oven. Remove foil and bake another 15 min.

APPLE PIE

FILLING INGREDIENTS

6 cups	thinly sliced Gala apples, peeled and cored
1 cup	sugar
$\frac{1}{3}$ cup	flour
¾ tsp	nutmeg
¾ tsp	cinnamon
½ tsp	salt
2 Tbsp	butter cut into chunks

PREPARATION

Follow instructions for Backberry Pie (see page 226) crust and baking procedures.

SURVIVAL COOKIES

INGREDIENTS

½ stick	butter
½ cup	canola oil
¼ cup	brown sugar
¼ cup	white sugar
½ tsp	vanilla extract
2	eggs
1¼ cups	flour
1 cup	old-fashioned oats
¼ tsp	baking soda
½ tsp	salt
¼ tsp	cinnamon
½ cup	dried cranberries
½ cup	chopped walnuts
½ cup	semisweet chocolate chips

PREPARATION

Heat canola oil and melt butter. Add sugars and whisk in vanilla and eggs. Add flour, oats, baking soda, salt, and cinnamon; mix well. Add nuts, cranberries and chocolate, stirring well. Drop each tablespoon of batter onto ungreased baking sheet, leaving a space between each cookie to allow for rising. Slightly flatten each mound of cookie dough/ Bake 13 minutes in preheated 325°F oven.

THE EVENING APERITIF

HUNTER'S HEARTH LIQUEUR

INGREDIENTS

3 bottles	cabernet sauvignon
1¾ cup	vodka
2 cup	sugar
1	lemon, thinly sliced
1	orange, thinly sliced
½	whole vanilla bean, sliced lengthwise

PREPARATION

Put sugar in large ceramic or stainless steel bowl. Add all other ingredients but DO NOT STIR.

Cover tightly with foil and then a tight lid. Stir 15 seconds once a day for 21 days, replacing tight cover each day. Remove citrus and vanilla bean with slotted spoon, then strain liqueur through cheesecloth. Bottle, cork, and refrigerate.

Ghost. The bird dog every upland gunner dreams of having.

Epilogue

Ghost and I just opened our fourteenth grouse season together. Mike was here, after missing last year with what he casually dismissed as "a mild stroke." Magoo fussed with his new shotgun and Heart. Eric Sharp made pictures.

I made everlasting memories.

The temperature was way too warm—in the low 70s—and the leaves were all very green. The brackern ferns were brown but not down, so watching the dog was difficult and tripping over dead tree limbs was a very real possibility.

But Ghost had a nose full of scent and she ran all over the place because she couldn't much hear me whistle for her when the breeze picked up.

Woodcock won't come into season for another ten days, which is unfortunate because of course she pointed three today and more or less looked at me with her sideways glare when I didn't shoot them.

She got her grouse, though. It was one of those half-crazed swamp birds, and I think he was nipping at all of those ripe viburnum berries, or perhaps wintergreen or huckleberry leaves, when Ghost found him.

She stopped and hunched forward when she first caught a whiff. Then came her patented "panther prowl"—each leg moving in slooooow motion until her nose was just so full of bird she couldn't take another step.

It was another one of those "magazine points." All classy with her feathery tail arched high, gently swaying in the breeze, and her left front foot pulled up. It was so damned pretty I nearly forgot to move in and flush the bird.

Mike coughed gently and Eric mumbled something I couldn't make out. Magoo was cleaning his eyeglasses. I remembered what we were there for, and that Ghost would be awfully mad at me if I blew this one, so I stepped forward and kicked the bird loose.

Brrrrrrr—it juked behind a cedar tree—rrrr—the Beretta's barrels poked toward a little opening—rrrr—there was an almost involuntary BANG and I watched the grouse fall. Ghost watched, too.

She got to it first, of course, and was holding it in her mouth, two steps from the river's edge. I patted her head, and hugged and kissed her just a little bit because we both were so happy.

She let me have the bird, and we admired it together for a few minutes. I stroked its rusty brown-phase plumage and spread the fan of its tail. She licked it and snorted in the heady aroma. We smiled at each other, then, as two old friends will do when a job's well done.

I put the bird in the pocket of my vest, held out an Alpo Snap for her to eat, and poured some water into the collapsible dish I carry. She drank a bit, then pawed at it as if she were digging a hole, splashing the little bit of remaining water over her chest and the toes of my boots. It was hot, and she was cooling off.

"Okay," she said after a shake that began at her white-capped left ear, traveled the length of her sleek body, and ended at the bloody tip of her magnificent tail. "Let's go get another one!" Then she smiled and stalked like a tiger toward a tangled mess of blackberry canes, dead branches, and tall weeds.

Damn, I'm a lucky man.